2 0 0 7

EFFECTIVE EDUCATIONAL PRACTICES FOR STUDENTS WITH AUTISM SPECTRUM DISORDERS

A RESOURCE GUIDE

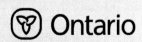

CONTENTS

ABOUT THIS GUIDE

1. FOUNDATIONS 9

Understanding Autism Spectrum Disorders 10
About Autism Spectrum Disorders 10
Terminology 11
ASD 12
Causes of ASD 13
Prevalence of ASD 14
Diagnosis of ASD 14
Characteristics of Students with ASD 15

Program Planning 18
Parent Involvement 18
Individual Learning Profile 22
Assessment 24
The Individual Education Plan (IEP) 28
Collaborative Planning 31
Universal Design for Learning 33
Planning for Transitions 36

2. TEACHING AND LEARNING 39

Instructional Strategies 40
Differentiated Instruction 40
Visual Supports 42
Structured Learning Environment 45
Assistive Technology 47

Une publication équivalente est disponible en français sous le titre suivant : *Pratiques pédagogiques efficaces pour les élèves atteints de troubles du spectre autistique.*

This publication is available on the Ministry of Education's website, at www.edu.gov.on.ca.

Sensory Considerations 49
Applied Behaviour Analysis (ABA) 52

Teaching Students with ASD 59
Literacy Skills 60
Mathematics 64
Homework 67

3. COMMUNICATION AND BEHAVIOUR   69

Behaviour Management 70
Managing Challenging Behaviour 70
Successful Practices for Behaviour Management 72

Communication 79
Communication Challenges Associated with ASD 79
Strategies to Develop and Enhance Communication Skills ... 81

Social Skills 89
The Development of Social Skills for Students with ASD 89
The Fundamentals of Social Skill Instruction 93
Strategies to Facilitate Social Understanding 98

About Asperger's Disorder 102
Challenges Associated with Asperger's Disorder 102
Strategies to Develop and Enhance Student Skills 106

4. TOOLS AND TECHNIQUES   109

APPENDICES

Appendix A: Glossary 208

Appendix B: Resources 209

Appendix C: References 211

ABOUT THIS GUIDE

As educators, we share a deep commitment to ensuring that every student has the opportunity to succeed and achieve to his or her highest potential. In developing this guide, the Ministry of Education acknowledges the valuable work being done in schools and classrooms across Ontario, and the dedication of teachers throughout the province to creating a learning environment that supports the success of every student.

What You Will Find in This Guide

This resource guide is designed to support educators in elementary and secondary schools in Ontario in planning and implementing effective educational programs for students with Autism Spectrum Disorders (ASD). It contains information, strategies, and practices that can be put to use in the school and the classroom. It also includes a collection of sample materials reflecting current practices in schools, as well as lists of references and resources for further reading.

Effective Educational Practices for Students with Autism Spectrum Disorders (ASD) includes the following elements:

- **Foundations:** General information about the diagnosis of ASD, characteristics of individuals with the disorder, and key principles for planning effective educational programs for students with ASD

- *Teaching and Learning:* Strategies and practices that have been found to be effective for students with ASD
- *Communication and Behaviour:* Strategies and techniques for addressing challenging behaviour, and improving communication and social skills
- *Tools & Techniques:* Sample materials that represent the most effective current practices, collected from school boards and regional autism service provider agencies across Ontario.
- *Reference Materials:* A glossary and lists of helpful resources on ASD, including publications and websites, as well as children's books.

Getting the Most from This Guide

Effective Educational Practices for Students with Autism Spectrum Disorders (ASD) is designed as a practical reference you can use every day. In order to get the most out of this guide, you may wish to read it first in its entirety. Then, you can refer back to specific chapters or sections, or select from the various samples provided in Chapter 4, "Tools and Techniques". As you explore the suggestions and tools provided in this guide, keep in mind that it is important to adapt them to the specific needs of the student, classroom, and school. *Individualized approach.*

Look for These Text Features

To make this guide as useful as possible, the following symbols have been designed to highlight key features within the text.

TIPS FOR TEACHERS
For quick reference on strategies that have been found to be effective

TOOLS & TECHNIQUES
From Ontario school boards and regional autism service provider agencies

INSIGHT
For deepening your understanding of ASD

KEY FACTS
For consideration in planning programs for students with ASD

RESOURCES
For additional information and further study

Deepening Your Knowledge

In recent years a wealth of information and resource materials has been developed regarding the education of students with ASD. This resource guide is not intended as a complete or comprehensive source of information, but has been developed to provide examples of practices that have been found to be effective. Educators who are seeking additional information for further investigations on the topic of educating students with ASD are encouraged to consult the references and resources listed in the appendices of this guide, and to monitor the growing body of knowledge on this topic.

Why This Guide Was Developed

The Ontario Ministry of Education has undertaken a number of initiatives to support school boards, school authorities, and provincial/demonstration schools in teaching students with ASD. In September 2003, the ministry organized a conference on teaching students with autism, in partnership with the Autism Society of Ontario (now Autism Ontario), the Geneva Centre for Autism, the Council of Ontario Directors of Education, and the Council for Exceptional Children. Following the conference, the ministry worked with Ontario school boards to provide regional forums, in French and English, for educators working directly with students with autism at the school level to further explore programming and effective teaching strategies.

In 2004, the School Support Program – Autism Spectrum Disorder (SSP–ASD) was established through a partnership between the Ministry of Children and Youth Services and the Ministry of Education, school boards, and designated community agencies. The SSP–ASD is administered by nine lead autism service provider agencies. Through this program, ASD consultants are connected with school boards to work with school staff – teachers, principals, and others who interact with children – to help them address the needs of students with ASD.

To complement the services available through the autism service provider agencies, the ministry funded Geneva Centre for Autism to provide training opportunities in the 2006-2007 and 2007-2008 school years for teachers' assistants (TAs) who work or may work with students with ASD.

In fall 2006, the Ministers' Autism Spectrum Disorders Reference Group was established to provide advice to the Minister of Education and the Minister of Children and Youth Services on effective, evidence-based educational practices to meet the wide range of needs of students with ASD. The reference group included practitioners, researchers, parent representatives, and representatives from the francophone community who were selected for their expertise and professional and personal experience with children, youth, and young adults with ASD. A report with recommendations from the reference group – *Making a Difference for Students with Autism Spectrum Disorders in Ontario Schools: From Evidence to Action* – was prepared for the ministers, and in spring 2007 the report was distributed to school boards.

In support of the recommendations of the reference group, in May 2007 the ministry released Policy/Program Memorandum No. 140, "Incorporating Methods of Applied Behaviour Analysis (ABA) into Programs for Students with Autism Spectrum Disorders (ASD)", 2007. Regional training sessions were offered to board teams to clarify the expectations in the PPM.

To build on all of the previous initiatives, the ministry has developed this resource guide as another step to support school boards in the education of students with ASD in elementary and secondary schools.

Acknowledgement

The Ministry of Education acknowledges the contributions of resources and information from Ontario school boards, the Geneva Centre for Autism, and the regional autism service provider agencies that deliver the School Support Program – Autism Spectrum Disorder, which were invaluable in the creation of this guide.

1 FOUNDATIONS

Autism Spectrum Disorders (ASD) are complex neurological disorders that have a lifelong effect on the development of various abilities and skills. Helping students to achieve to their highest potential requires both an understanding of ASD and its characteristics, and the elements of successful program planning required to address them.

IN THIS CHAPTER

Understanding Autism Spectrum Disorders

About Autism Spectrum Disorders	10
Terminology	11
ASD	12
Causes of ASD	13
Prevalence of ASD	14
Diagnosis of ASD	14
Characteristics of Students with ASD	15

Program Planning

Parent Involvement	18
Individual Learning Profile	22
Assessment	24
The Individual Education Plan (IEP)	28
Collaborative Planning	31
Universal Design for Learning	33
Planning for Transitions	36

Understanding Autism Spectrum Disorders

About Autism Spectrum Disorders

Autism Spectrum Disorders (ASD) are complex neurological disorders that have a lifelong effect on the development of various abilities and skills. ASD is characterized by impairments in communication and social interaction, as well as unusual patterns of behaviours, interests, and activities.

The term "spectrum" is used to recognize a range of disorders that include a continuum of developmental severity. The symptoms of ASD can range from mild to severe impairments in several areas of development. Many professionals in the medical, educational, and vocational fields are still discovering how ASD affects people and how to work effectively with individuals with ASD.

MYTHS ABOUT ASD	THE FACTS
ASD is rare.	ASD is not rare. It affects approximately **1 in every 165 persons** (Fombonne et al., 2006).
ASD is an emotional disorder.	ASD is a **neurological** disorder.
Poor parenting causes ASD.	Parents do **not** cause ASD in children.
There is a cure for ASD, or children will "grow out of" the disorders.	Children do **not** grow out of ASD. With early intervention and good educational programs, students may make significant progress.
Everyone with ASD behaves in the same way.	Students with ASD are **individuals** who each have unique strengths and needs.
Students with ASD have to be in special programs for "the autistic".	Individually designed programs best meet the needs of students affected by ASD. Students need to be learning, living, and working in settings where there are ample opportunities to communicate and interact with others who have the skills they need.
(Adapted with permission from the website of the Geneva Centre for Autism, April 2006)	

KEY FACTS

Terminology

The terms "autism", "Pervasive Developmental Disorders (PDD)", and "ASD" have been used interchangeably within the literature and by professionals and parents, and may cause confusion.

Autism was first identified in 1943 by Leo Kanner, an American psychologist. Kanner noticed distinctive, common characteristics within a subgroup of children in whom other mental disorders had been diagnosed originally. Kanner recognized the inability of this subgroup to relate in the ordinary way to other people and situations, and he described this behaviour as "extreme autistic aloneness" (Kanner, 1943). As a result, for several decades the disorder was referred to as autism.

KEY FACTS

Autism is recognized by the Ontario Ministry of Education as a communication exceptionality for the purposes of student identification and placement. This term continues to be used frequently as a shorthand term to include various conditions that are now recognized as a range of disorders.

The general term "PPD" is often confused with the specific diagnosis of PDD NOS.

Pervasive Developmental Disorders (PDD) was first used in the *Diagnostic and Statistical Manual of Mental Disorders–III (DSM-III)* by the American Psychiatric Association (APA) in 1980 as a general term to describe a class of disorders that shared the following characteristics: impairments in social interaction, imaginative activity, and verbal and non-verbal communication skills, and a limited number of interests and activities that tend to be repetitive. In 1994, five disorders were identified in the updated *DSM-IV* (APA, 1994) under the category of PDD: Autistic Disorder, Rett's Disorder, Childhood Disintegrative Disorder, Asperger's Disorder, and Pervasive Developmental Disorder Not Otherwise Specified (PDD NOS).

Autism Spectrum Disorders (ASD) was first used in 1988 (Wing, Allen) and is now commonly used to describe a subset of PDD that includes only Autistic Disorder, Asperger's Disorder, and PDD NOS. In some cases, the term ASD is used to acknowledge the complete range or spectrum of associated characteristics and disorders that are included in PDD.

The term "ASD" will be used throughout this document in reference to students who have Autistic Disorder, Asperger's Disorder, or PDD NOS.

ASD

The following is a brief summary of each of the three disorders considered ASD. More specific information regarding the diagnostic criteria, such as the characteristics that must be present in both quantity and type for diagnosis, can be found in the *Diagnostic and Statistical Manual of Mental Disorders-IV Text Revision (DSM-IV-TR)* (APA, 2000).

Autistic Disorder

Students with Autistic Disorder have noticeably abnormal or impaired development in social interaction and communication and a restricted repertoire of activity and interests. Such students often show a preoccupation with one narrow interest and an insistence on following routines. Abnormalities in the development of cognitive skills and in posture and body movements may be present. These impairments are accompanied by a delay or abnormal functioning in social interaction, language used in social communication, or symbolic or imaginative play that was recognized prior to three years of age.

Asperger's Disorder

Like students with Autistic Disorder, students with Asperger's Disorder show impaired social interaction and display a limited field of interests and activities prior to three years of age. This impairment causes difficulties in social and/or occupational functioning. The difference between students with Autistic

Disorder and Asperger's Disorder is that students with Asperger's Disorder show no significant delay in language acquisition, although the more subtle aspects of social communication may be affected. There are no significant delays in cognitive development or in the acquisition of age-appropriate learning skills or adaptive behaviours. Restricted, repetitive patterns of behaviour, interests, and activities are common. Students with Asperger's Disorder may experience feelings of social isolation, which may contribute to depression or anxiety in adolescence.

Pervasive Developmental Disorder Not Otherwise Specified (PDD NOS)

Students with PDD NOS have severe impairments in the development of reciprocal social interaction, including impairments in either verbal or non-verbal communication skills, or have stereotyped behaviours, interests, and activities. PDD NOS, also referred to as "atypical autism", includes individuals who do not fit into the other categories because they do not meet all of the diagnostic criteria for a specific disorder; for example, diagnostic symptoms may occur at a later age.

Causes of ASD

There are several theories about the cause or causes of ASD. Researchers are exploring various explanations but, to date, no definitive answers or specific causes have been linked scientifically to the onset of ASD. Research suggests that individuals with ASD experience biological or neurological differences in the brain.

In many families, there appears to be a pattern of ASD-related disabilities, which suggests that ASD is an inherited genetic disorder. Current research studies show that certain classes of genes may be involved or work in combination to cause ASD. There appear to be many different forms of genetic susceptibility but, to date, no single gene has been directly related to ASD (Autism Genome Project Consortium, 2007). Ongoing research is being done to further investigate the cause of ASD.

KEY FACTS

It is important to note that ASD is not a mental illness, and there are no known psychological factors in the development of the child that have been shown to cause ASD.

Prevalence of ASD

ASD was once viewed as a rare disorder, but recent studies suggest that the prevalence rate for all forms of ASD is much higher than previously thought. The most current estimates from studies in Canada and the United Kingdom are that ASD is diagnosed in 60 of every 10,000 children, or one in 165 (Fombonne et al., 2006).

ASD is now recognized as the most common neurological disorder (Geneva Centre for Autism, 2006) and has been found throughout the world in families of all racial, ethnic, and social backgrounds. It is diagnosed more frequently in males than females; worldwide, males are affected four times as often as females (Chakrabarti & Fombonne, 2005).

An increase in the numbers of individuals in whom ASD is diagnosed can be linked to a combination of factors. With the broader definition of PDD that was provided in *DSM-IV* (APA, 1994) and an improved recognition of the symptoms, changes in diagnostic practices have occurred (Chakrabarti & Fombonne, 2005). As a result, the diagnosis of PDD is being made more frequently and at an earlier age (Fombonne, 2003). Also, in recent years, more rigorous methods are being used in surveys to find and gather data on cases of ASD.

While other possible causes for the increasing rates of diagnosis and resulting identification continue to be investigated, there is no direct evidence to support an increased incidence, or epidemic, of ASD. The research cited above suggests that ASD appears to be more common now because the tools used for diagnosing ASD in children are better now than before.

Diagnosis of ASD

The complex nature of ASD makes it difficult to diagnose, and there is no single medical test to determine if a student has ASD. In general, the perspectives of various professionals are required as part of the diagnostic process, which usually includes an assessment conducted by a qualified professional

KEY FACTS

ASD in Ontario
In the 2005-06 school year, school boards in Ontario reported that 7,888 students in publicly funded elementary and secondary schools were identified by an Identification, Placement and Review Committee (IPRC) as exceptional under the Communication–Autism category. This is more than double the 3,348 students who were reported to be identified in the same category in the 1998-99 school year (Ontario Ministry of Education, School October Reports).

who specializes in developmental disorders, such as a child psychiatrist, developmental pediatrician, child psychologist, or neuropsychologist.

Accurately diagnosing ASD in a student typically includes the following:
• assessments of multiple areas of functioning, such as intellectual and communication skills
• a review of developmental history
• parental input

Diagnosis is not a quick process and is much like putting together pieces of a puzzle. ASD is diagnosed through the presence or absence of certain behaviours, characteristic symptoms, or developmental delays. Often several tests may be performed to rule out other medical conditions, such as a loss of hearing that may be causing the social and communication impairments, before considering a diagnosis of ASD.

In many cases, ASD will be diagnosed in children before they begin attending school, often when they are between two and three years of age, although in some cases the child will start school prior to receiving a medical diagnosis of ASD. Parents often share with health professionals the information provided by educators about concerns related to the development of a child's social, communication, and behaviour skills in the school setting. This information may assist in the determination of an appropriate medical diagnosis.

Characteristics of Students with ASD

Several disorders are included in the diagnosis of ASD, and the symptoms and characteristics of each disorder can be present in a variety of combinations and develop within a continuum of severity. The degree of impairments can range from mild to profound and will affect individuals very differently.

Characteristics vary widely. For example, some students may be overly sensitive and display extreme reactions to sensory stimuli,

TOOLS & TECHNIQUES
See Chapter 4:
1. Online Autism Modules
2. Information Pamphlet
  for Administrators

while others do not respond at all to the same stimuli. Also, although students with ASD generally have impairments in both verbal and non-verbal communication skills, those with Asperger's Disorder usually have relatively good verbal skills.

KEY FACTS

There is no single impairment, behaviour, or ability level that identifies ASD. Although ASD is typically characterized by impairments in communication and social interaction, as well as unusual patterns of behaviours, interests, and activities, the extent of the difficulties will vary considerably across individuals and within an individual over time.
(National Research Council, 2001)

The following chart describes some characteristics, related to the above-noted impairments, that students with ASD may exhibit in the classroom.

INSIGHT

CHARACTERISTICS OF ASD AS SEEN IN THE CLASSROOM	
Area of Impairment	**The student:**
Social skills	• demonstrates difficulties interacting with peers and adults • has difficulty reading and understanding social cues or situations • withdraws from or provides unusual responses in social situations • engages in play that is lacking in the imaginative qualities of social play
Communication skills	• has difficulty communicating thoughts and needs verbally and non-verbally • has difficulty with non-verbal communication, such as use of gestures, pictures, eye contact, and facial expressions • uses speech that includes repetitive, echolalic, or unusual language
Behaviour	• displays obsessions or preoccupations with specific themes or objects • likes order and may line up toys repeatedly • engages in unusual behaviours, such as rocking, spinning, or hand flapping • gets extremely upset with changes in routine or schedules • has an unusual response to loud noises or other sensory stimuli

The general level of intelligence can vary significantly across the population of students with ASD. Some individuals will demonstrate normal levels of cognitive development, while others will have profoundly impaired or abnormal development of cognitive skills. For example, about 75 per cent to 80 per cent of individuals with Autistic Disorder will have significant cognitive impairments. Many individuals with Asperger's Disorder, however, will have average to above-average intellectual functioning (Perry & Condillac, 2003).

The profile of various cognitive abilities in an individual may also be uneven, regardless of the individual's general level of intelligence. In some cases, special or "splinter" skills are present: an individual has highly developed skills in a very specific area of ability, such as long-term memory, but the same individual also has severe impairments in the development of other skills. For example, some individuals with Autistic Disorder may have excellent recall of technical data or mathematical formulas, but they repeat the information over and over again in a context that is socially inappropriate.

In many cases, comorbid (or additional) disorders, such as an anxiety or mental disorder, are diagnosed in individuals with ASD. The effects of the symptoms of other disorders can increase the severity of impairments for individuals with ASD.

Program Planning

TOOLS & TECHNIQUES

See Chapter 4:
3. Survey for Parents

KEY FACTS

Ontario Regulation 181/98, *Identification and Placement of Exceptional Pupils*, requires the principal, in developing the individual education plan, to consult with the parent and, where the pupil is age 16 or older, the pupil (Clause 6 (6)(a)).

Parent Involvement

Parents play a vital role in the education of their children. As partners in the process, parents can provide perspectives and information that will broaden educators' understanding of the student. Parent participation will enhance program planning and assist in the determination of educational goals, methods, and motivational strategies that are most appropriate and effective for a student.

A consultative partnership between home and school is developed through regular, frequent opportunities for discussions about the student's unique learning needs, evidence of progress, and any adjustments to the educational program that may need to be considered.

Students with ASD generally have difficulty transferring or generalizing skills from one situation or environment to another. The learning process for a student with ASD is supported when the same skills and concepts are reinforced in both the home and school environments.

Involving families in planning their child's educational program may assist in developing the student's ability to learn. Families are often able to provide additional opportunities for the student to practise skills. This may also enhance the student's ability to generalize skills to various settings. Students will be more successful in learning and generalizing skills when families and schools share a common focus, approach, and goals.

Having a child with ASD is a challenge for any family and may have an emotional, physical, and financial impact on the family (Higgins, Bailey, & Pearce, 2005). The impact on families can vary considerably across situations. Some families are able to cope with these additional stressors; however, for others it can be more difficult. It is important to keep in mind that many parents are on their own journey of acceptance of the diagnosis and its significant implications for both their own lives and the life of their child.

The needs of families who have children with ASD can depend on:
- the particular characteristics of their child (such as age, level of functioning);
- the parents' own interpersonal resources;
- the availability and effectiveness of supports and services.

When interacting with families, it is important to be sensitive to these issues (Perry & Condillac, 2003).

Parents are able to provide valuable information about many key aspects that affect how a student participates at school, such as:
- Developmental history
- Health issues
- The range of professionals who are or have been involved with the student and the services provided
- Their child's likes, dislikes, special interests, and sensory sensitivities
- Effective positive reinforcers and motivators
- How the student has learned skills at home
- Behaviour and communication strategies that have been successful at home and in other environments
- Student performance across settings and over different periods of time
- Perspectives on the student's personality.

Teachers should secure appropriate consents from parents regarding personal information about students.

TIPS FOR TEACHERS

Parents are advocates for their child's best interests. It is essential that they have opportunities to be involved as partners in the ongoing planning and review of educational programs for students with ASD. A strong partnership between schools and families is the foundation for a student's ongoing, successful experience at school.

Home/School Communication

Positive relationships between home and school have been shown to improve parental involvement and increase parents' comfort level in working with the school.

It is important to keep in mind that home/school communication for many students with ASD is a method of reporting for students who, because of the nature of their disability, cannot do this for themselves.

TOOLS & TECHNIQUES

See Chapter 4:
4. Student's Day at School
5. School Communication

The nature of the communication between home and school can have a significant impact on the quality of this relationship, as well as on a student's program at school and the ongoing development and generalization of skills. Many parents report that they wait expectantly to read the communication book at the end of each day and that their emotional state can be considerably influenced by its content. Thus, it is important to be cognizant of the messages that are sent and how the messages are stated.

It is important that the teacher, TA, principal, and parent meet to discuss and establish methods for home/school communication. Consideration should be given to the format, information to be included, information from home that will be shared, and the constraints of time for all parties. As well, guidelines for reporting any significant behavioural issues need to be clearly established.

The classroom teacher is responsible for the content of the home/school communication. In some situations, while a TA may guide the student through the process of reporting daily events, this should be reviewed by the teacher. As a guideline to positive practice, the teacher should use methods such as a home/school communication book or phone call to maintain contact with the parent on a regular basis to provide updates on the student's activities and progress.

Generally, parents want to know about the activities in which their child participated during the day. Parents can use this information to talk with their child and elicit communicative responses whenever possible. Information to assist in this process can include:

- Activities in which the student participated
- Any new or particular skills that were demonstrated
- Nature of play with friends and classmates

- Songs and stories of the day
- New themes or areas of learning
- Upcoming, special events, trips, or snack days.

TIPS FOR TEACHERS

Health Issues

Some children have serious health issues, such as seizures or allergies, about which parents need more frequent information. Any serious occurrence should be reported to parents immediately. Collaboration between parent and school is essential to mutually decide on a way to report on health-related issues that is efficient for both home and school. In any situation where health issues are a serious concern, safety protocols must be created and shared with all staff.

Reporting Behavioural Difficulties

Most parents are aware of the behavioural difficulties of their child, and it can be a disheartening process to regularly receive a listing of their child's misbehaviours throughout the day. In most situations, it is unnecessary to report the daily incidences of non-compliance, off-task behaviour, and other occurrences if these are an ongoing or typical component of the child's behavioural profile.

Remember to report positive information as often as possible. This can have a significant impact on the quality of a family's evening or weekend.

There will be times when reporting and discussion of behaviour are necessary and unavoidable. When significant behavioural incidents occur, they must be reported to parents. However, the communication book is *not* the forum for sharing this kind of information. The principal decides how this information is to be shared with parents, and often assumes this important role.

In composing the content of daily communication, it can be helpful to ask yourself these questions: What if the communication book became lost and was found by another student or a stranger? Would the child's or the family's dignity or privacy be compromised?

Establishing a Successful Home/School Communication Process

- Involve the student in creating the system. Students can be partners in preparing pictures or picture symbols, writing, stamping, or applying stickers in the home/school communication book. This gives the student a sense of ownership and responsibility for the process.
- Often, the job of writing in the communication book is left until the end of the day. In some cases, however, it is possible to connect the student's visual schedule to the daily home reporting process. This method is helpful to reinforce the schedule and involve the student directly in communication with parents. Make the reporting process as positive as possible. The preparation and maintenance of the communication book can be a valuable component of the literacy program for some students.
- Respect the privacy of families.
- Comments should be objective. Always imagine yourself in the position of the parent receiving the information.
- When possible, pictures of the student involved in school activities can provide an excellent stimulus for information retrieval and communication. Reviewing pictures of school activities while at home will help some students to generalize thinking between the home and school environments.

While it will take a few extra minutes each week to manage the home/school communication process, the responsive and responsible reporting of the events of a student's days at school makes a positive contribution to both the home and the school experience. Parents feel informed, supported, and more able to support the learning needs of their child.

TOOLS & TECHNIQUES

*See Chapter 4:
6. Information Pamphlet
on ASD*

Individual Learning Profile

Decisions about what to teach or how to teach an individual student should not be based solely on the diagnosis of ASD. No one method or intervention will meet the needs of all students with ASD, as individual students differ in their abilities and their needs vary considerably (National Research Council, 2001).

Some students with ASD may have developmental delays or an intellectual disability and experience challenges with a number of basic, pre-learning, developmental skills, including imitation, joint attention, and generalization, while others may have much more highly developed skills. Program planning for students with ASD, as for all students with special education needs, should be individualized and focused on developing skills that will be of use in the student's current and future life in school, home, and community. This requires careful planning, preparation, and teamwork so that the programs provided are appropriate and effective for the individual student.

Determining the educational interventions that may be required to meet the learning needs of students with ASD begins with an understanding of the unique learning profile of each student. This requires consideration of information from a range of sources, such as the following:

- data and reports from assessments
- observations of skills and behaviours through the student's participation in assignments, activities, tasks, and projects
- Ontario Student Record (OSR)
- information and reports provided by parents, former teachers, and other involved professionals, such as service providers from outside the school system

In developing the learning profile for a student with ASD, it is important to consider information gained from observations of the student. Observations should be as objective and descriptive as possible and avoid value judgements. In particular, educators should note the student's:

- progress towards learning outcomes;
- behaviours and interactions that occur in the school and classroom environment, including recess and lunchtime;
- age and social appropriateness of interactions with peers and adults;
- social language skills;
- reactions to the learning environment and the setup of the classroom;
- responses to transitions in the school day – between activities in the classroom, for example.

TOOLS & TECHNIQUES

See Chapter 4:
7. Critical Information Sheet
8. Student Profile
9. Promoting Independence

Unusual developmental profiles are common for students with ASD, and therefore careful documentation of a student's unique strengths and weaknesses is necessary and can have a major impact on the design of effective intervention programs.

Assessment

Assessment information from various sources will need to be considered to develop individual learning profiles and establish appropriate educational programs for students with ASD. Comprehensive assessments are necessary to recognize and understand the various strengths and needs of individual students. It is important that generalizations or unrealistic expectations about overall abilities are not made on the basis of the diagnosis, individual skill impairments, or splinter skills.

Assessment data and results that have been gathered across a diverse range of skills by a variety of professionals will provide comprehensive information that will be useful in making accurate decisions about programs for students. A diagnosis of ASD is associated with impairments in communication, social, and behavioural skills, and multidisciplinary assessments in these skill areas will provide information that will be used to determine the extent of the impairments and how the difficulties interfere with the educational process.

When a student in whom ASD is diagnosed is first enrolled in school, parents should be invited to participate in a transition planning process that includes the sharing of any relevant assessment information with the school. This information will be considered in:
- determining the student's strengths and needs;
- deciding learning goals for the student;
- making decisions regarding programs, services, and supports that may be required to meet the student's needs;
- establishing records against which to measure future achievement.

Parents should be encouraged to participate in an ongoing process of sharing any relevant, updated assessment information with the school.

KEY FACTS

Policy/Program Memorandum No. 11, "Early Identification of Children's Learning Needs", 1982, requires school boards to have procedures to identify each child's level of development, learning abilities, and needs. A continuous assessment and program planning process should be initiated when a child is first enrolled in school and continue throughout the child's school life.

Assessment of student progress by a classroom teacher is a continuous, complex process that is an integral part of the learning-teaching process every day. Teachers use a variety of methods to gather information about a student's achievement, the level of the student's understanding, and the effectiveness of a particular teaching technique. Examples of classroom-based assessment methods that are used by teachers on a regular basis to assess student learning include the following:

- observations
- teacher-designed tasks
- interviews with the student
- criterion-referenced academic tests
- functional assessments

See Chapter 4:
10. Inventory of Functional
Skills

During the school day, there are ongoing opportunities for teachers to assess students across a variety of settings and situations. The information and data collected by teachers are primarily used for planning programs that will be appropriate to each student's strengths, interests, needs, and level of functioning.

The choice of assessment instruments is a complex one and depends on the student's:

- verbal skills;
- ability to respond to complex instructions and social expectations;
- ability to work rapidly;
- ability to cope with transitions in test activities.

(National Research Council, 2001:28)

The responsiveness of a student with ASD to an assessment task may be affected by the novelty and structure of the assessment situation. Consideration should be given to the possibility that the results of an assessment may indicate the student's response to the assessment task or situation and may not be an accurate reflection of the student's abilities.

Assessment accommodations may be required to allow the student with ASD the opportunity to demonstrate achievement of specific skills or expectations. Examples of assessment accommodations that may be required for students with ASD include providing:

- visual supports to clarify verbal instructions;
- additional time for student responses;
- alternative methods for the student to demonstrate achievement of skills;
- alternative environments for assessment tasks.

TIPS FOR TEACHERS

It is important to consider the following when assessing the academic skills of students with ASD:

- Recognize that verbal responses may be the most difficult and least accurate.
- If a verbal response is required, do not insist on eye contact.
- Provide the student with methods to answer questions non-verbally, if possible. For example, provide Yes/No or True/False cards that the student can touch or point out to indicate the answer.
- Allow the student several readings of a passage before asking comprehension questions.

This may include reading the passage to the student.

- Begin an assessment process by starting with material two or more grades below the ability level of the student. Gradually work up to the student's level.
- Provide the student with sample questions to practise with the assessment format.
- Allow the student to answer questions using the computer.

An effective assessment process is continuous and includes ongoing, systematic data collection that is necessary to:

- monitor student progress;
- evaluate instructional effectiveness;
- update goals as a student learns and masters a skill.

Information about skill development in multiple areas of functioning should be considered when decisions are made about students' programs. This would include collecting and analysing data and other information related to progress within various skill areas such as communication, social, and behavioural skills, in addition to academic skills. For example, students with ASD often exhibit behaviours that are unusual or disruptive to the learning process. A systematic assessment process such as a functional behaviour assessment should be followed to determine the purpose of the behaviour, identify contextual factors that may be triggering the unusual or problematic behaviour, and evaluate the effectiveness of intervention strategies. Further information about functional behaviour assessments is found in Chapter 3 of this guide.

Multidisciplinary assessments include those conducted by qualified professionals, such as psychologists, speech-language pathologists (SLPs), and occupational therapists (OTs) who are staff within the school board or from the Ministry of Health and Long-Term Care, such as OTs from Community Care Access Centres (CCACs). In many cases, parents obtain assessments for their children from external institutions, agencies, or practitioners and provide consent for this information to be shared with the school.

Assessment information from various sources will provide valuable information to guide the development of the student's Individual Education Plan (IEP) and assist in the continuous process to determine educationally relevant goals, objectives, and implementation strategies that are based on the unique learning profile of the individual student.

 Further information regarding assessment of students with special education needs can be found in *Special Education: A Guide for Educators* (Ontario Ministry of Education, 2001) and *Education for All: The Report of the Expert Panel on Literacy and Numeracy Instruction for Students With Special Education Needs, Kindergarten to Grade 6* (Ontario Ministry of Education, 2005a).

The Individual Education Plan (IEP)

Many students with ASD will be identified by an Identification, Placement and Review Committee (IPRC) as exceptional students under the Communication–Autism category. As described in *Special Education: A Guide for Educators* (Ontario Ministry of Education, 2001), the definition that the IPRC considers in determining the exceptionality of Communication–Autism is:

A severe learning disorder that is characterized by:
a) *disturbances in:*
  • *rate of educational development*
  • *ability to relate to the environment*
  • *mobility*
  • *perception, speech, and language*
b) *lack of representational symbolic behaviour that precedes language.*

The IPRC will determine the most appropriate placement to meet the individual needs of students with ASD who are identified as exceptional pupils. Parents and students (if 16 years of age or older) are invited to attend the IPRC meetings and participate in the committee discussions. A range of placement options and services should be available for students with ASD to address the broad range of needs of these students. The needs of many students with ASD are met in regular class placements with appropriate supports. Other students require placement in special education classes for all or part of the school day.

The IEP is a written program plan that describes the special education program and/or services required by a student on the basis of a thorough assessment and understanding of the student's strengths and needs. The information gathered to understand a student's individual learning profile will be an important resource in the development of an appropriate program plan for the student. The IEP should be reviewed and updated regularly, at least once in every reporting period, and based on ongoing and continuous evaluation of the student's progress.

Most students with ASD have special education needs that need to be considered in an Individual Education Plan (IEP). This includes students who have been identified as exceptional by an IPRC, and also students who may have received a diagnosis of a disorder within the range of ASD but may not be formally identified by an IPRC as an exceptional pupil.

The IEP is a working document that identifies the accommodations that are required to help the individual student achieve learning expectations and demonstrate learning. The IEP also identifies the modified or alternative learning expectations, where appropriate, that are planned for a student's educational program and the specific knowledge and skills to be assessed and evaluated for the purpose of reporting student achievement.

It is helpful, for purposes of planning and IEP development, to classify the subjects or courses and alternative programs in which the student will receive instruction according to the following categories, as appropriate to the student's individual requirements:
- No accommodations or modifications
- Accommodated only
- Modified and/or
- Alternative.

KEY FACTS

Accommodations are the special teaching and assessment strategies, human supports and/or individualized equipment required to enable a student to learn and demonstrate learning. Accommodations do not alter the provincial curriculum expectations for the grade.
Modified expectations differ in some way from the regular grade expectations as outlined in the Ministry of Education's curriculum policy documents.
Alternative expectations are developed to help students acquire knowledge and skills that are not represented in the Ontario curriculum.
(*The Individual Education Plan (IEP): A Resource Guide*, Ontario Ministry of Education, 2004)

For some students with ASD, the most appropriate program is based on expectations from the Ontario curriculum with minimal or moderate accommodations or modifications. Other students may require a program that includes significantly modified expectations or is mainly composed of expectations that are an alternative to the Ontario curriculum. Educational goals for students with ASD often need to address social, communication, and adaptive skills that are not part of standard curricula (National Research Council, 2001). For many students with ASD, the most effective education program includes a combination of instructional goals based on the Ontario curriculum with accommodations or modifications, as required, and includes alternative programs with specific goals and activities to support the development of functional skills that are useful and meaningful for the student.

Parents and relevant school board and community personnel who have previously worked with and/or are currently working with the student should be invited to provide input and participate in the IEP process. This may include, but is not limited to, consultations with current and previous teachers, the principal, the student, a psychologist, special education staff, an OT, service providers from community agencies, and autism program providers, as appropriate.

All members of the IEP team have important roles and responsibilities in the IEP process. It is important that the teacher(s) responsible for the direct instruction and assessment of the student's progress work collaboratively with parents and other involved professionals to determine the student's programming needs and appropriate learning expectations.

Effective educational programming for students with ASD should be based on a student's abilities and gradually increase in complexity as skills develop. In order to achieve this, programs should be carefully planned and constantly evaluated using a variety of formal and informal assessments. The program should then be modified on the basis of assessment results and student progress.

For additional information on the IEP process in general, refer to *Individual Education Plans: Standards for Development, Program Planning, and Implementation* (Ontario Ministry of Education, 2000), and *The Individual Education Plan (IEP): A Resource Guide* (Ontario Ministry of Education, 2004).

Collaborative Planning

A collaborative planning approach to support students with ASD is most effective and promotes the best outcomes for students. Keeping this in mind, it is important for school staff to invite input from and the participation of the parent(s) and, with parental consent, other professionals who have previously worked with and those who are currently working with the student. Students with ASD have a broad range of needs and abilities. The perspectives, information, and resources from parents and various in-school, school board, and community professionals will enhance the effectiveness of the program planning process.

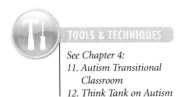

See Chapter 4:
11. Autism Transitional
*   Classroom*
12. Think Tank on Autism

Many school boards in Ontario have established school-based support teams that play a significant role in helping teachers to plan and implement programs for students with special learning needs. The school team is made up of school staff members who work together with the family to collaborate, consult, and share information and knowledge to identify strategies that may increase the student's learning success. As circumstances require, the team may also seek assistance from other resources, such as the following:
- community associations and agencies (such as Autism Ontario)
- service providers from the Ministry of Health and Long-Term Care (such as CCACs, which coordinate service providers such as OTs)
- service providers from the Ministry of Children and Youth Services (such as staff of the regional autism service provider agencies)
- Children's Treatment Centres (CTCs)
- Children's Mental Health Centres

Multidisciplinary teams composed of professionals with expertise in a variety of areas have also been developed by some school boards to provide additional support to schools in the planning

See Chapter 4:
13. Resources for Drivers
14. Transportation Visuals

of effective programs for students with ASD. The membership of the multidisciplinary team could include a consultant, an SLP, a psychologist, an OT, and others who have the experience and knowledge to provide information, resources, and recommendations related to meeting the needs of students with ASD.

Through working collaboratively with other individuals, staff are able to better understand a student's learning profile and become aware of interventions that have successfully supported other students or the student in other environments. With this knowledge, staff can plan appropriate program goals and interventions for the student.

Some school boards have found it helpful to develop protocols with local community agencies to identify responsibilities and processes for working together. These local agreements are used to support collaborative partnerships by identifying and resolving issues that may arise. Collaborative efforts will be enhanced and most effective when those involved are committed to working together for the best interests of the student.

Students with ASD often experience difficulty with change. Establishing consistent practices is promoted through collaborative planning and may help to alleviate some of the challenges for students during transitions such as entry to school and between grades. Education strategies and practices are most effective if they are implemented across various settings, including the home, school, and community (Iovannone et al., 2003).

Universal Design for Learning

Education for All (Ontario Ministry of Education, 2005a), provides educators with recommendations on a broad range of techniques to enhance the instruction of students with special education needs, including those with ASD.

The report provides information on the use of the principles of Universal Design for Learning (UDL) and differentiated instruction to plan for and respond to students with various needs. Learning is a continuum and every student is a unique learner. Flexible, supportive, and adjustable classrooms and programs must be planned and developed to meet the learning needs of individual students. These are important considerations in the planning of programs for students with ASD.

UDL is recommended for consideration by teachers to guide the planning of the various components of teaching, such as defining the expectations of learning situations and determining the teaching strategies and assessment methods that will be required. Programs designed according to the core concepts of UDL are based on considerations of the following:
- universality and equity
- flexibility and inclusion
- an appropriately designed space
- simplicity
- safety

Universality and Equity
Teachers are encouraged to develop a class profile to identify the strengths, challenges, and needs of all students and to determine the stage that each student has reached in his or her learning. The instructional methods and classroom accommodations should be planned to ensure that the needs of all students are met.

TOOLS & TECHNIQUES

See Chapter 4:
15. Autism Demonstration
   Site
16. Strategies Checklist

For additional information on Universal Design for Learning, see *Education for All: The Report of the Expert Panel on Literacy and Numeracy Instruction for Students With Special Education Needs, Kindergarten to Grade 6* (Ontario Ministry of Education, 2005a).

Students with ASD vary in their cognitive level, communication ability, social skills, and behavioural characteristics. They have a wide range of skills and diverse needs. It is important for teachers to gather information to understand the individual strengths, needs, and interests of students to identify appropriate curriculum expectations, required accommodations, and effective instructional approaches.

Flexibility and Inclusion

To ensure that all students are provided opportunities for real learning experiences, flexibility and options should be built into the planning of teaching strategies, materials, and student activities.

The ability of students with ASD to participate in or respond to a learning experience may be affected by limitations in communication and social skills. Consideration of the likes, dislikes, strengths, needs, and interests of a student with ASD can help to make materials and tasks more engaging and provide motivation for the student to participate in and complete the desired task or activity. Concrete examples and hands-on activities provide students with opportunities to learn by seeing and doing and have been found to increase the motivation and engagement levels of students with ASD. For example, a student who has difficulty with concepts in mathematics may be motivated to learn graphing techniques by gathering data on items of personal or special interest.

Student engagement increases the learning opportunities for the student and has been found to be one of the best predictors of positive student outcomes (Iovannone et al., 2003).

Many students with ASD have difficulty processing information and are unable to respond immediately and "on demand" to expected tasks. They often require flexibility regarding the timing and method used to demonstrate their knowledge and skills. Teachers will need to consider the various alternatives, such as extended timelines and additional activities that may need to be planned to ensure that appropriate learning experiences are provided for all students.

An Appropriately Designed Space

Consideration should be given to the size, space, and arrangement of the physical and visual elements in the learning environment to ensure that they are conducive to student learning.

Students with ASD may be unusually sensitive to sensory stimulation, which can be reflected in an increased sensitivity to the physical environment of the learning situation. The classroom is filled with many sensory demands that can be overwhelming for some students. Although some of these demands, such as noise in the hallway and fire alarms, are unpredictable, teachers should monitor the physical environment to ensure that the sensory distractions (such as auditory and visual stimuli) for a student with ASD are minimized as much as possible. For example, tennis balls can be used to cover the bottoms of chair legs to reduce classroom noise.

TOOLS & TECHNIQUES

See Chapter 4:
17. Classroom Layout
18. Morning Routine

Some students with ASD are very aware of and need to know where things belong. The organization of materials, furniture, and resources should be carefully considered in relation to their effect on the learning environment of the student with ASD.

Simplicity

Teachers should ensure that the information provided in learning situations is presented clearly and is easily understood by the students. Unnecessarily complex and distracting information should be reduced as much as possible.

The communication impairments that are often present in students with ASD may affect their ability to process verbal information. They will often have difficulty understanding complex, abstract language and may misinterpret metaphors, slang terms, and colloquialisms. Effective methods to simplify information and make it easier for the student to understand include using clear and concise language, breaking instructions and tasks into smaller steps, and using visual supports, such as written or picture schedules. Information and materials should be organized in such a way that important or key components are highlighted and easily identified by students.

See Chapter 4:
19. Safety Plan: Crisis
    Protocol
20. Information for
    Occasional Teachers

Safety

Teachers need to consider possible safety hazards and elements with the potential to cause accidents in the classroom. Staff should be aware of and able to act on any safety assessments, safety plans, or safety protocols that may apply to specific students in the classroom.

If a student with ASD is considered to be a safety risk in the school setting, adults involved with the student need to have access to the information and supports that are required to ensure a safe learning environment. A safety assessment can help to identify the factors that may lead to or cause situations and provide an assessment of the potential risks in given situations. A safety plan outlines the appropriate responses and supports that are required during specific situations with students.

Planning for Transitions

Common characteristics associated with a diagnosis of ASD are restricted, repetitive patterns of behaviour, interests, and activities. Many individuals with ASD have difficulty coping with novel and unexpected events. Change, including transitions between activities and environments, is often difficult for students with ASD and can lead to increased anxiety and unusual or inappropriate behaviours.

See Chapter 4:
21. Suggestions to Support
    Transitions
22. Preparing Students for
    a Special Event

In school, transitions happen at various stages and levels for students. Some transitions occur on a regular basis between activities and settings within the routines of the school day. Other transitions, such as class excursions, occur less frequently. Significant transitions such as entry to school, between grades and divisions, from elementary to secondary school, and from secondary school to the postsecondary destination happen periodically, are more complex, and include significant changes to many aspects of a student's routines.

Planning for transitions provides the foundations for successful transition experiences that help a student learn to cope with change and adapt to a variety of settings. Transitions cannot be avoided, but helping a student to be prepared for and adjust to change and transition can help to reduce or avoid some of the anxiety and unusual or inappropriate behaviours that they may cause.

FACILITATING TRANSITIONS

To facilitate transitions:	Examples
Begin preparing the student well in advance of the expected transition.	• A calendar is used daily to count down the days until a class trip. • Pictures and stories of the trip destination are reviewed for several days prior to the trip.
Plan transition steps to allow the student to gradually become familiar with change.	• A schedule of visits is arranged for the student to adjust to the new school. Scheduled timelines and things to see are increased for each visit.
Use consistent cues or routines to signal transitions.	• A "transition object" is carried by student during the move to the next class. • The same song or phrase is heard by student before the start of a routine activity.

TIPS FOR TEACHERS

Transition planning for students with ASD should begin well in advance of the expected change for the student. The planning can be complex and requires communication and coordination between those who will be involved in the transition process. Effective planning for significant transitions usually includes parents and staff from the school, school board, and community agencies who are and who will be involved with the student.

For additional information on transition planning, see:
- Ontario Regulation 181/98, *Identification and Placement of Exceptional Pupils*
- *Individual Education Plans: Standards for Development, Program Planning, and Implementation* (Ontario Ministry of Education, 2000)
- *Transition Planning: A Resource Guide* (Ontario Ministry of Education, 2002)
- *The Individual Education Plan (IEP): A Resource Guide* (Ontario Ministry of Education, 2004)
- *Planning Entry to School: A Resource Guide* (Ontario Ministry of Education, 2005b).
- Policy/Program Memorandum No. 140, "Incorporating Methods of Applied Behaviour Analysis (ABA) into Programs for Students with Autism Spectrum Disorders (ASD)", 2007 (Ontario Ministry of Education, 2007a).

TOOLS & TECHNIQUES

See Chapter 4:
23. Task Sequence for Home Time
24. Visuals for Transition from School to Home

Parents should be involved in the sharing of information, collaboration, planning, and process that may be required to ease or facilitate significant transitions for a student. Parents can help to identify changes to routines or settings that may be difficult for the student. They can also help to support successful transitions by assisting in determining an effective transition process for an individual student or building skills and/or routines to familiarize the student with different expectations in the new setting.

The purpose of transition planning is to determine the considerations, goals, and actions that will be required to support the student in making a positive transition to the new setting and experiences. It also provides an opportunity for those within the new setting to become familiar with and prepare for the student.

2 | TEACHING AND LEARNING

A wide range of strategies and approaches is available to support the teaching and learning process for students with ASD. Integrating a variety of approaches leads to the development of programs that promote the best outcomes for students.

IN THIS CHAPTER

Instructional Strategies

Differentiated Instruction	40
Visual Supports	42
Structured Learning Environment	45
Assistive Technology	47
Sensory Considerations	49
Applied Behaviour Analysis (ABA)	52

Teaching Students with ASD

Literacy Skills	60
Mathematics	64
Homework	67

INSTRUCTIONAL STRATEGIES

*[handwritten: *Variety of approaches based on individualized needs.]*

The National Research Council (2001) found that no one specific method or intervention is effective for all individuals with ASD and that integrating a variety of approaches leads to the development of programs that promote the best outcomes for students.

Differentiated Instruction

As recommended in *Education for All* (Ontario Ministry of Education, 2005a), teachers can effectively respond to a learner's needs and strengths through the use of differentiated instruction. Through this approach, the specific skills or difficulties of students with ASD can be addressed by employing a variety of methods to differentiate (or vary) the following:

The content: The depth or breadth of the information or skills to be taught.

The processes: The instructional approaches used with the student, as well as the materials used to deliver or illustrate the content.

The products of the learning situation: What the end product will be or look like. This product may be tangible (a worksheet, project, composition), a skill that has been acquired, or knowledge that has been gained.

To determine the most effective strategies for students in a learning situation, it is necessary to consider the learning goals for the student in the context of the following questions:

- **What** do we want the student to learn? What essential skills or understandings do we want the student to acquire?
- **Why** is the student learning this? How does the learning goal fit into the goals outlined in the IEP for the student?
- **How** will the student best learn this? What type of activities, materials, and supports are appropriate and effective for the student? How will the student demonstrate learning?

To differentiate instruction, teachers should consider adaptations to the curriculum, instruction, or expectations that may be required according to a student's readiness, interests, and learning profile.

DIFFERENTIATED INSTRUCTION	
Elements that can be varied to differentiate learning activities	**Examples of differentiation for students with ASD**
Student groupings	• Establish multiple or similar ability grouping. *peers* • Divide groups according to similar interests. • Clearly define the role for each student in a group (e.g., note-taker, reporter, artist).
Instruction activities	• Support verbal information with visuals. • Include explicit (or direct) teaching of information. • Provide opportunities for the student to practise and rehearse.
Level and type of support provided to the student	• Include tasks that the student can participate in or complete independently. • Provide opportunities for peer support through small-group activities. *peers.* • Have more intensive levels of assistance available as required.
Task expectations (time, type of task)	• Build in flexible or extended timelines for task participation and completion. • Chunk longer activity into smaller segments (e.g., divide a 45-minute activity into several shorter sections). • Encourage use of technology to complete a task (e.g., keyboarding for written tasks).
Materials and resources	• Match materials and resources to the readiness level, interests, and learning profiles of students (e.g., a student with keen interest in vehicles collects data on cars in a parking lot and graphs results).
Assessment activities	• Provide a variety of opportunities and ways for the student to demonstrate learning. • Allow alternatives to written tasks, such as drawings, fill-in-the-blank activities, questions with multiple-choice answers, pointing to the correct answers, scribing. • Include visual supports such as graphic organizers or highlighting of key words.

TIPS FOR TEACHERS

Differentiation involves an ongoing process of monitoring student response to the differentiated strategies and evaluating student progress on a regular basis. Strategies that are found to be effective for a student during one activity may be less effective over time or during another activity. The level and type of differentiation will need to be varied according to the student's response and progress. Data from assessments and observations should be used to inform decisions about the effectiveness of methods being used and further differentiation that may be required.

Visual Supports

The use of visual supports is one of the most widely recommended strategies for teaching students with ASD, as they usually process visual information more efficiently and effectively than information that is presented verbally. Some students may require extra time to process verbal language and understand the message. Speech is transient: once information or instructions have been spoken, the message is no longer available and students must recall the information from memory.

Visual images help students to understand information as they provide a source that can be referred to as often as necessary and for the length of time that is required in order to process the content of the information.

Visuals are mainly used to:
- *Improve communication:* provide a reminder or cue of what to say or do in a situation *(social interaction.)*
- *Provide information:* supplement or provide an alternative to verbal information

TOOLS & TECHNIQUES

See Chapter 4:
25. *Visual Steps for Using Workout Room*
26. *Visuals for School Activities*
27. *Visuals for Going to Work*

For additional information on differentiated instruction, see *Education for All: The Report of the Expert Panel on Literacy and Numeracy Instruction for Students With Special Education Needs, Kindergarten to Grade 6* (Ontario Ministry of Education, 2005a).

- *Support routines:* provide a method to organize or schedule the sequence of activities
- *Teach skills:* clearly delineate content or skill expectations and become a source that can be referred to as required (socials?)
- *Prevent problems:* present choices and behavioural alternatives
- *Intervene when there is a problem:* provide a clear, consistent, familiar response

(Hodgdon, 1999; Quill, 1995)

VISUALS	
Purpose of visual	**Examples of visual supports**
Prompt for transitions	Visual schedule, card with symbol of next activity
Provide directions or instructions	List of written expectations
Break tasks into easier to understand steps	Series of pictures to demonstrate steps required
Provide structure and predictability to routines and activities within the student's day	Daily schedule or calendar
Assist in organizing the environment	Labelled objects
Support appropriate behaviour	Cue cards (e.g., STOP), stories, or written behavioural routines and expectations
Develop choice-making skills	Choice board with pictures of options, or a written list for students who have reading skills

TIPS FOR TEACHERS

43

"There is a behaviour-communication-visual link:

- *The **causes** of behaviour difficulties are frequently related to communication difficulties: problems in understanding and/or difficulty with expression.*
- *The **remedy** to improve behaviour is improving communication.*
- *The **method** is using visual strategies to support communication."*

(Hodgdon, 1999)

When planning an activity, it is important to consider ways the information can be presented in a simple, visual format that may be effective for a student with ASD to comprehend.

Heirarchy of Visual Supports
Real objects
Miniature objects
Colour photographs
Black & white photographs
Colour picture symbols
Black & white line drawings
Printed words

Visual supports can vary according to the ability of the student to recognize and understand the connection between the visual and the intended message.

In order for visual aids to successfully help a student to learn, they must match the student's level of comprehension. Some students require very basic, concrete visual objects while others understand and respond to more abstract symbols or written language. Using line drawings or symbols for a student who can comprehend only real objects will cause frustrations for both the student and the teacher. The visuals being used must be easily and quickly recognized by the student. The goal of using visuals is to help a student understand or convey information. Visual supports are helpful to many sudents with ASD, including those who are able to read efficiently.

Social initiations?

Visual supports can include visual schedules, checklists, task exemplar sheets, choice boards, illustrated task sequences, printed instructions, rules or topical/content materials, tip sheets, safety signs and messages, videos, and story illustrations, as well as illustrations based on theme content (e.g., the Pioneer Unit).

These are two effective methods of visual support:

1. **Passive modelling** (Biederman et al., 1998): Students are able to see what is expected in a task by being provided with visual examples and demonstrations of how tasks are performed. Instructional language is reduced as much as possible.
2. **Video modelling** (Bellini & Akullian, 2007): Further to and building on the concept of passive modelling, video modelling *social initiations?* provides the students with a video example of how tasks are performed and task sequences. This format allows the student to watch the instructional sequence over and over.

In terms of practice, both passive modelling and video modelling are viable tools. Through the use of a digital camera, short instructional sequences on CD-ROMs can be prepared quickly and easily. These sequences can be a powerful addition to other instructional methods and materials.

TOOLS & TECHNIQUES

See Chapter 4:
28. Bus Rules
29. Getting Ready for the Bus
30. Individualized Daily Schedule

Visual supports are usually simple and inexpensive. They will be most effective for a student with ASD if they are used consistently and across various settings. For example, a visual schedule used at home to organize the after-school activities for a student will be easier for the student to understand and use if it is referred to daily and follows a format similar to the one used at school to structure the student's school day.

Structured Learning Environment

All children function better in a predictable environment. Students with ASD require a structured learning environment to know what is expected of them in specific situations, to assist them in anticipating what comes next, and to learn and generalize a variety of skills (Iovannone et al., 2003). Rules and expectations should be clear and consistent and include specific information regarding the expectations for appropriate behaviour.

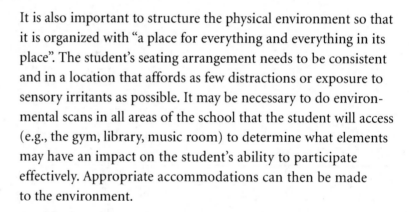

Strategies for structuring the learning environment for a student with ASD include:

- Posting the student's individual rules or guidelines, as well as classroom rules, in a visually accessible location (e.g., beside the student's desk or workspace)
- Providing clear information about task expectations
- Introducing new or unfamiliar tasks in a familiar environment

- Establishing routines and regularly scheduled activities
- Developing a visual schedule of activities
- Providing warnings before transitions or changes to routines
- Having specific places where materials are stored
- Following a consistent work system.

It is also important to structure the physical environment so that it is organized with "a place for everything and everything in its place". The student's seating arrangement needs to be consistent and in a location that affords as few distractions or exposure to sensory irritants as possible. It may be necessary to do environmental scans in all areas of the school that the student will access (e.g., the gym, library, music room) to determine what elements may have an impact on the student's ability to participate effectively. Appropriate accommodations can then be made to the environment.

TOOLS & TECHNIQUES

See Chapter 4:
31. Monday Schedule
32. Classroom/Environment
33. Ten Ways to Create
*   Classroom Structure*

Developing as much consistency as possible in the environment, schedule, and instructional approaches provides structure and routines that may increase the comfort level and reduce anxiety for students with ASD. However, there are situations in which changes to the environment and routines during the school day are inevitable. Providing students with what they need to be prepared for these changes, such as advance warnings and concrete visual information, can help them to become more flexible and adaptable to change. Once students know the expectations of their visual schedule and transition system, flexibility training can be built into the process.

Recording changes in the student's visual schedule and providing opportunities for the student to rehearse and review upcoming changes have been found to be effective in preparing students with ASD for changes to the learning environment and routines.

For example, if the student's regularly scheduled gym class is cancelled because the gym is being used for another activity, the student will need preparation to understand this change. The change could be explained to the student and visually recorded in the student's daily schedule with an alternative activity, ideally one that is highly preferred by the student. Involving the student in making the change to the visual schedule and visiting the gym to see the other activity being set up may help the student to understand the change.

Students with ASD are most successful in an organized environment that is structured to be as predictable and understandable as possible.

Assistive Technology

See Chapter 4:
34. Selecting Student
Organizers

In *Education for All* (Ontario Ministry of Education, 2005a), assistive technology is defined as any technology that allows one to increase, maintain, or improve the functional capabilities of an individual with special learning needs (Edyburn, 2000). Its applications and adaptations can help open doors to previously inaccessible learning opportunities for many children with special needs (Judge, 2001).

Assistive technology includes highly technical (commonly referred to as "high-tech") computerized devices such as speech generating software, as well as less technical ("low-tech") resources such as visual supports. Technology can be used by students to provide alternative methods to access information, demonstrate and reinforce learning, and interact with others. It can also be used ★social interaction by adults as a tool to support the teaching and learning process.

A research study investigating the use of assistive technology with students with ASD in British Columbia (Randle, 2005) used a survey to identify a wide variety of uses of technology that include supporting the following:

- written output
- academic concept development
- motivation
- communication
- the development of social skills

TIPS FOR TEACHERS

The survey responses from school-based teams in a study on the use of assistive technology with students with ASD in British Columbia indicated that successful implementation of technology appears to depend on several factors such as:

- Match between the technology and the student's need
- Positive attitude towards the student's use of technology to access learning
- Interest and comfort level of the teacher and TA in using technology
- Reliable and timely access to technical support, when required
- Student comfort level in using technology with gradual introduction of new hardware and/or software, when required
- Perseverance through problems and challenges.

As the learning needs of students with ASD are diverse, it is important that a student's specific technological needs be evaluated and that the use of assistive technology be carefully planned. The potential benefits of assistive technology for individual students should be considered from a multidisciplinary and cross-curricular perspective. For example, technology that is used to support a student's communication skills may also be found helpful to accommodate a student's fine motor difficulties and increase written output.

The support that is provided through the use of assistive technology will change over time for a student and may vary across activities. For example, a student may require the use of text-to-speech software to support the understanding of information in one subject area, but may not require it to read and understand materials on a topic of interest.

Special Equipment Amount Funding

Special Equipment Amount (SEA) funding assists school boards with the costs of equipment that is not available through the board's normal textbook, supply, and/or computer purchasing arrangements. Equipment funded through SEA must be recommended by a qualified professional to be essential to support students with special needs and provide students with accommodations to access the Ontario curriculum and/or a board-determined alternative program and/or course and/or to attend school. Evidence of the use of equipment must be documented in the student's IEP. For additional information on Special Equipment Amount funding, see *Special Education Funding Guidelines: Special Equipment Amount (SEA) and Special Incidence Portion (SIP), 2007–08* (Ontario Ministry of Education, 2007b).

Ongoing monitoring of students' needs and use of assistive technology is important to determine if the technology is being used effectively and is providing the student with the intended support. Collaboration between parents and professionals will help to ensure that the technology that is being used is appropriate to meet the needs of the student and is as multi-functional as possible.

Sensory Considerations

Students with ASD vary in their sensitivity and tolerance to sensory stimulation in the environment. It is important to be aware of the sensory preferences or sensitivities of a student and to determine possible elements in the environment that might have an impact on a student's learning and level of anxiety.

Some students are very ("hyper-") sensitive in one or more sensory areas and may be more comfortable in environments with reduced levels of sensory stimulation. Other individuals are under ("hypo-") sensitive and seek enhanced sensory experience. For example, some students become anxious or upset because of an extreme sensitivity to certain sounds or have a difficulty processing more than one sense at a time. Other students seek additional sensory experiences in order to become or maintain calm.

It is usually possible to determine strategies or accommodations that are effective to manage sensory issues. In some cases, environmental accommodations can be made quite easily. In others, students can be taught socially appropriate ways to access sensory materials and experiences. Proactive strategies to manage sensory issues include:

- providing predictable, scheduled breaks for sensory input;
- providing a variety of sensory materials and/or equipment that will mitigate a student's particular sensory needs;
- using engagement in sensory activities as reinforcement for task completion and other classroom requirements or expectations;
- performing environmental scans across all environments in a school that the student may access in order to determine possible sensory irritants and make adjustments accommodations as appropriate.

Parents are a valuable resource in providing detailed information about their child's sensory issues. OTs are usually involved in determining the sensory-based activities and materials that will enable a student to regulate his or her arousal level and associated behaviour.

UNDERSTANDING SENSORY BEHAVIOURS

Sensory Domain	Hyposensitivity (Seeking Behaviour)	Intervention Strategies	Hypersensitivity (Avoidance Behaviour)	Intervention Strategies
Visual	The student likes to look at spinning objects, flicks fingers, rocks, is attracted to lights	Schedule times in the day for the student to have access to visually stimulating materials	The student closes eyes, rubs eyes, is attentive to details, has good visual memory	Maintain visually well-organized environment, ensure visual clarity within tasks
Auditory	The student enjoys noisy environment, machines, running water, flushing, loud music	Provide headphones for listening to music, access to musical instruments, environmental sound CDs	The student makes repetitive noises, avoids specific sounds, is a light sleeper	Provide headphones to block sounds; encourage student to listen to soft, peaceful music; provide a quiet workspace

INSIGHT

Sensory Domain	Hyposensitivity (Seeking Behaviour)	Intervention Strategies	Hypersensitivity (Avoidance Behaviour)	Intervention Strategies
Tactile (Touch)	The student likes to touch people and things, bumps into others, may be self-injurious, has little reaction to pain	Provide items with a variety of tactile qualities, e.g., koosh ball, sand, water, velvet, satin	The student may tolerate a limited number of fabrics, resists physical contact, is upset by crowds	Accommodate clothing issues to the extent possible, respect personal space and comfort level
Olfactory (Smell)	The student may try to smell people and things	Provide a "Smelly Book" (spices, flavourings, etc.) as a reward or leisure activity	The student avoids people and places (e.g., washroom) that have an odour	Provide an alternative item to smell in difficult locations, provide access to a different washroom, never wear perfume
Gustatory (Taste)	The student may ingest inappropriate objects, likes strong tastes, may focus on particular foods	Schedule specific times for food to be eaten, do not focus on food variety as a necessity, consider nutritional value	The student prefers bland foods, has active gag reflex, tastes foods cautiously	Consult with the parents to see if a nutritionist or other professional is involved
Vestibular (Balance and movement)	The student enjoys and needs movement; may enjoy spinning, jumping, and bouncing	Provide opportunities for gross motor activity and access to equipment (trampoline, rocking chair, etc.)	The student may have low muscle tone, avoids gym equipment and movement, has difficulties with balance	Obtain input from an OT, if necessary, to assist in creating a strength-building program; provide opportunities for movement
Proprioceptive (Awareness of the body and its spatial boundaries)	The student seeks deep pressure, asks for or seeks hugs, walks on toes, grinds teeth or chews inedible things	Consult with an OT regarding items to provide pressure (weighted vest, stress ball, etc.), schedule physical activities (jumping, running, etc.), accommodate need for tight-fitting clothing	The student has poor body awareness, avoids pressure, appears to be clumsy and weak	Provide opportunities for swimming and other exercise

INSIGHT

Applied Behaviour Analysis (ABA)

As outlined in Policy/Program Memorandum No. 140, "Incorporating Methods of Applied Behaviour Analysis (ABA) into Programs for Students with Autism Spectrum Disorders (ASD)", 2007, ABA is an effective approach to understanding and changing behaviour, and teaching new skills. ABA uses methods based on scientific principles of learning and behaviour to build useful repertoires and reduce problematic ones. In this approach, the behaviour(s) to be changed are clearly defined and recorded, and the antecedents and reinforcers that might be maintaining an undesirable behaviour, or that could be used to help develop alternative or new behaviours, are analysed. Interventions based on principles of learning and behaviour are then designed and implemented to develop appropriate behaviours. Progress is assessed and the program is altered if necessary (adapted from Perry, A. & Condillac, R., 2003).

ABA can be used as an instructional approach with students of every age. It can be applied in a variety of situations, and it can be employed for very limited and specific purposes such as the development or reduction of single behaviours or sets of behaviours. ABA methods can be used with varying degrees of intensity along a student learning continuum. ABA is used according to the individual needs of each student, and may be applied to developing academic skills or behaviours related to social skills, communication, or self-care.

social

The focus in an instructional approach that uses ABA is on measuring and tracking behaviours over time, determining the function of the target behaviour (for the student), and altering the behaviour (either increasing or decreasing its occurrence) by providing intervention. Student progress is based on ongoing data collection and assessment, as measured against the identified objectives. The ultimate goal of using ABA methods is the generalization of the learned skills and behaviours to other settings and situations.

ABA methods can be used to:
- increase positive behaviours;
- teach new skills;
- maintain behaviours;
- generalize or transfer behaviour from one situation to another;
- restrict or narrow conditions under which interfering behaviour occurs.

In practice, using methods of ABA involves a number of discrete steps:

Step 1: *Clearly define the behaviour to be changed and the goals and objectives for changing the student's behaviour. It is important to focus on behaviours that can be observed, measured, and tracked over time.*

Step 2: *Evaluate and record current levels of performance for the targeted skills and behaviours to establish a baseline.*

Step 3: *Design and implement appropriate interventions. Interventions should be based on an analysis of the antecedents (what comes before behaviour) and reinforcers (what comes after behaviour) that might be maintaining undesirable behaviours or that could be used to help develop alternative (or adaptive) behaviours. A functional behaviour assessment (FBA) is an effective means to determine the underlying function or purpose of behaviours (see "Managing Challenging Behaviours" in Chapter 3 of this guide).*

Step 4: *Continue measuring the target behaviours to determine if the intervention is effective, and if additional skills or behaviours need to be targeted.*

Step 5: *Undertake an ongoing evaluation of effectiveness, and make necessary adjustments to maintain or increase the effectiveness of interventions.*

Examples of teaching strategies using ABA methods include prompts, modelling, reinforcement, task analysis, forward chaining, backward chaining, Discrete Trial Training, and shaping. These are discussed below.

Prompts: Prompts are cues or assistance to encourage the student to provide the desired response. There are many natural prompts in the environment, for example, seeing the school bus

social?

53

arrive, hearing a bell ring, or noticing that students are lining up at the door.

Prompts can be:
- direct ("Put your books on the shelf in the locker") or indirect ("Where do books need to go?");
- verbal, physical, or visual (gestures or pictures);
- brief (to get the student started on a task) or intensive (step-by-step through the task).

TOOLS & TECHNIQUES

See Chapter 4:
35. How to Prompt
36. Prompt Tracking Sheet
37. Prompts Used in
*   Initiating Play*

Some students have difficulty recognizing, understanding, or responding to some prompts. It is important to determine the type and intensity of prompting that the individual student requires. Students can become dependent on prompts from others, so it is important to plan for the fading of prompts when appropriate. Visual supports can provide a method of prompting that many students can learn to use independently. Here, the goal is to help the student become as independent as possible in participating and completing tasks.

Modelling: A form of prompting is modelling. It provides a visual example of what is expected in a task by having students see the task being performed. It can also help the student see the sequence of steps in the task. For example, the student learns the actions to a song by first watching a demonstration by an adult.

social?

Reinforcement: The target behaviour is encouraged through the use of reinforcement. Reinforcement is provided after the target behaviour to increase the likelihood that the behaviour will reoccur. Reinforcers can be:
- tangible (such as stickers);
- activity-based (the student is able to participate in preferred activity);
- social (praise or thumbs up sign). *social interaction*

Reinforcement can be provided for displaying positive behaviours – to encourage these behaviours to continue – or for refraining from or reducing the occurrence of negative behaviours. It can be something provided (such as praise) or something removed (such as a non-preferred activity being removed when the student asks appropriately).

TOOLS & TECHNIQUES

See Chapter 4:
38. Following Directions
39. Interest Inventory
40. Reinforcement Inventory
  by Parent
41. Reinforcement Inventory
  for Elementary Student

Reinforcements must be motivating to the individual student. What motivates one student may not motivate another. Similarly, what is motivating to an individual student may change over time. It is important that monitoring be used to ensure that the reinforcer remains effective. In some cases, developing a "menu" of reinforcers may be helpful so that students may select from several options.

To encourage students to be as independent as possible, it is important to gradually change reinforcers from others to more natural reinforcers, such as the satisfaction of completing a task.

Task analysis: Task analysis involves breaking tasks down into smaller, teachable steps. Here, the goals for each step are established, and task performance can then be taught according to these steps. Each subtask is taught and reinforced in sequence. In many cases, students may have difficulty only with one step within the larger task, rather than with the task overall. It is important to write subtasks in terms of what the student will do, and to record interventions or prompting that are required for students to complete the subtasks.

Forward chaining: When steps within a task are identified through task analysis, use forward chaining to focus instruction to teach the first step or subtask that the student has not mastered, and then assist the student with the rest of the task. Once the student masters the first subtask, then focus instruction on the next step that the student has not mastered, continuing until the student can complete all of the subtasks. For example, in learning to print his or her name, focus the student on learning to print the first letter, and print the rest of letters for the student.

Backward chaining: In backward chaining, it is the last step or subtask that a student has not mastered that is focused on first. This provides the student with immediate reinforcement through successful completion of the task. Once this skill is mastered, the focus moves to the next-to-last subtask. For example, a student learning to remove outdoor clothing might initially focus on learning to hang his or her coat on a coat hook after being assisted with other steps. Next, the student would learn to take off his or her coat, and then hang it on the hook.

Discrete Trial Training (DTT): Like task analysis, DTT involves analysing skills and breaking large tasks into steps or subtasks (or discrete skills). Here, subtasks are usually taught sequentially, and each subtask is mastered before learning the next skill. DTT consists of four steps:

See Chapter 4:
42. Giving Praise Effectively
43. Reinforcer Chart

1. The student is given a brief instruction or question (stimulus) that is designed to produce a specific response. If necessary, the instruction is followed by a prompt.
2. The student responds.
3. If the response is as expected, the student receives reinforcement such as praise.
   If the response is not as expected, the response is ignored or corrected or the student is prompted to provide the expected response.
4. Data are recorded.

Subsequent trials or instructions are then given.

Shaping: Shaping involves the use of reinforcements to change behaviour gradually and systematically. Here, approximations of the desired behaviour are reinforced until the target behaviour is achieved. For example, these steps could be followed if the target behaviour is for the student to sit with a group during storytime:

- Step 1: reinforcement for standing near the group
- Step 2: reinforcement for standing closer to the group
- Step 3: reinforcement for standing in the group
- Step 4: reinforcement for sitting in the group

social

ABA can be used to understand and change behaviour and teach new skills in a variety of ways.

Purpose of ABA	Example of Desired Behaviour or Skill	Sample Method to Change Behaviour or Skill
Increase positive behaviours	To increase on-task behaviours	The student is allowed to select a preferred activity as reinforcement after working on a target activity. Data are collected to measure on-task behaviours and record reinforcements.
Teach new skills	To teach the student a motor skill such as throwing a ball	Step-by step-instruction based on a systematic task analysis is provided, using modelling and forward chaining. Praise is provided as reinforcement. Progression of skill development is measured and used to determine whether additional subtasks need to be targeted.
Maintain behaviours	To maintain the student's focus on the task	A student who becomes distracted from tasks and is upset when other students finish tasks is systematically taught and prompted to use relaxation techniques, such as deep breathing, as a method to maintain focus on the task.
Generalize or transfer behaviour	To generalize use of a skill that is used in a specific setting to other locations	Shaping and reinforcements are used to gradually and systematically encourage self-calming techniques that are effective in the resource room to be used on the playground. Data are collected to monitor use and effectiveness of self-calming techniques in other locations.
Restrict or narrow conditions under which behaviour occurs	To reduce use of inappropriate language	Through the use of Discrete Trial Training and reinforcement, the student learns to replace shouting of inappropriate words with more appropriate language. Data are collected to determine the use of replacement language and to track prompts required.

INSIGHT

The methods of ABA that are used within educational programs should be varied according to the strengths and needs of individual students, and the types of behaviours and skills that need to be taught. Some students may require intensive use of some of the above strategies within their program, while others may require the use of ABA as an instructional approach only for very limited, specific purposes. Each student's pattern of strengths and needs must be analysed to determine the specific learning objectives and teaching methods that are required and most appropriate.

peers ?

Effective use of ABA methods requires collaboration among parents, educators, and other involved professionals to determine appropriate goals and strategies for achieving them. Collaborative efforts provide opportunities for the generalization of new skills and behaviours across a variety of settings and situations.

Teaching Students with ASD

See Chapter 4:
44. Ten Recommendations

Integrating a variety of approaches leads to the development of programs that promote the best outcomes for students. Educational programs for students with ASD are developed through a process of information gathering and consultations to determine the individual learning profile for each student. For many students with ASD, the most appropriate educational program includes a combination of academic goals based on the Ontario curriculum with accommodations or modifications, as required, as well as alternative program goals to support the development of behaviour, communication, social, and functional living skills that are useful and meaningful for the student. The learning profiles for students with ASD are diverse and one specific method or program will not be appropriate for all students with ASD.

social

A growing body of research indicates that the following essential instructional components are important when instructing students with special needs (*including those with ASD*):

- Instruction must be of ***sufficient duration and intensity*** to produce adequate learning and application to new situations
- Students with special needs benefit from ***cumulative review*** of important concepts and skills
- Students with special needs require ***guided practice*** to help them bridge the gap between what they know and don't know, and they need to receive explicit instruction in how to apply learned information in new situations

- Teachers need to monitor their ***instructional language*** (both oral and written)
- Instruction needs to ***integrate both foundation skills and higher-order processes*** concurrently for students to be able to apply their knowledge and skills
- Students benefit from clear, organized teaching that ***makes explicit connections*** across previous and current content areas (*Education for All*, Ontario Ministry of Education, 2005a).

Literacy Skills

Reading

Many students with ASD have strong visual skills and are often more successful in learning to read through a whole word sight recognition approach than through a more traditional phonics program. Whole words that are meaningful are usually easier for students to learn to read than words for which students have no basis of experience or knowledge. In the beginning stages of learning to read, it is critical to enable students to develop a sense of confidence.

While knowing the alphabet and knowing the sound symbol associations are usually regarded as prerequisite skills for learning to read, many students with ASD often have difficulty acquiring these prerequisite skills (Mirenda, 2003). Some students are able to recite alphabet letters and letter sounds by rote, but may be unable to apply this to decoding words in a fluent manner. The rate of reading fluency will affect a student's ability to comprehend the message of the words. If a student needs to give more cognitive attention to a difficult decoding process, then it is likely that the student's understanding of what the words are saying will decrease.

See Chapter 4:
45. Visual Lotto Game
46. Visual Sentence Strip

Some students may be better able to understand and learn the phonetic components of words after they have learned to read them through a whole word sight recognition approach, working backwards within a top-down framework from the whole to the parts. It is important to consider that, although some students may be unable to manipulate the symbolic representations of sounds, they may still be able to recognize and comprehend words and acquire skills in phonics.

As the student acquires more words, it is essential to provide activities in which these words are used in meaningful contexts. Ongoing practice in sentence construction enables the student to understand how words are organized to express thoughts and needs, as well as how pronouns, articles, and prepositions are used in context. Daily practice in sentence construction provides students with the opportunity to develop an understanding of grammar and to learn a framework for using language. This practice also reinforces that repetition and rehearsal of language construction are ongoing expectations of daily task performance.

It is important to consider that while some students may not read aloud, they may be able to read and comprehend complex words and passages. It is necessary to provide the student with a variety of opportunities to demonstrate reading ability. For example:

- *Students who do not respond when asked to read a passage aloud may be able to select and match pictures related to the words or sentences.*
- *Manual signs can be paired with printed words and used to indicate word recognition for students who are non-verbal or emergently verbal.*

It is essential that students learn to recognize and read words across the curriculum. Reading cannot be confined to reading period, as it is a critical component of every subject area. Subject-specific vocabulary should be taught as one of the components of participation in the curriculum. Key vocabulary for a theme or unit should be determined and then reviewed and reinforced to help students generalize their recognition of the words. Key words can be recorded in a personal dictionary, scrapbook, or theme book, for example, "My Science Words", and, when possible, paired with pictures so that the visual concept is associated with the printed word.

The following strategies help to build literacy skills:

- As students acquire and consolidate sight word recognition skills, add new words to their vocabulary, gradually working from the names of people, objects, and places of interest to vocabulary associated with the curriculum and the environment.
- Use activities, games, and software to develop and reinforce letter knowledge, phonemic awareness, and grapheme-phoneme relations.
- Provide students with software (e.g., word prediction, word processor) to support writing efforts.
- Provide content and stories of interest that will further develop sight vocabulary.
- Allow for repeated reading of familiar text as this can facilitate fluency and comprehension.

- Include activities to highlight connections between words (e.g., rhyming games, word families, word sorting).
- Provide explicit instruction on decoding "rules" for spelling patterns. Encourage the use of rote memory skills for correct spelling, as well as attempts to use understanding of sound/symbol associations. Provide regular opportunities for practice.
- Use literacy skills to develop and enhance other skills, such as communication and social skills (e.g., talking word processor "reads" to classmates a story written by student).

Reading comprehension difficulties are common for students with ASD. Although some students develop an extensive reading vocabulary through whole word sight recognition or through a strong ability to phonetically decode previously unseen words, they may not be able to comprehend what they are able to read. Students' motivation to read and comprehension levels are likely to be increased when the vocabulary and storylines are familiar and meaningful. Initially, when students first engage in reading, stories created about family life, pets, favourite television characters, and similar topics will be far more relevant than stories about things, people, and places that are unfamiliar.

Many students with ASD have difficulty with the perception and understanding of sequences. This may lead to a significant challenge in the development of comprehension skills, as understanding causality and making inferences and predictions will be difficult. This difficulty can apply to sequencing skills in both daily life and in reading fiction and non-fiction. Activities such as using picture cards that can be sequenced to create a story or using if/then matching cards help students to develop skills in

perceiving, understanding, and creating sequences. Picture cards
that are relevant to the student's experiences, such as pictures of *peers .*
the student or familiar peers engaged in activities of interest to the
student, will be most effective. Illustrations from materials read
can be used to help the student sequence events and information.

Writing

While some students with ASD are proficient in printing and
handwriting, many others have difficulty with written tasks
because of difficulties with fine motor skills. The visual-motor
coordination and fine motor movements that are required in
written activities may be extremely frustrating and divert the
student's attention from the content of what he is writing to the
physical process of print production. Difficulties with handwriting
have been identified as one of the most significant barriers to
academic participation for students with ASD in schools today
(Simpson, 2007).

There are many ways in which technology can be used to enhance
and compensate for the limitations that students have in their
writing skills. If fine motor skills are a barrier to participation and
academic function, then seek the alternative of assistive technology.

The use of keyboards, word processors, and writing software
has facilitated the writing process for many students with ASD.
Learning to use a keyboard is a valuable skill for students to
acquire. For many students with ASD, using a computer is a highly
preferred activity. Teach and encourage the student to learn to
use the keyboard as a writing instrument. This is a reasonable
accommodation to the motor planning difficulties often associated
with ASD. While learning to print can be a useful exercise for many,
when students' difficulties with penmanship inhibit their ability
to demonstrate their knowledge and spark behavioural upsets,
the use of the keyboard is a viable alternative.

In many cases, OTs are involved with students with ASD and
provide assessments and information on a student's fine motor
and writing skills. OTs can provide recommendations about the
strategies, resources, and accommodations that will be appropriate

to assist students with fine motor and writing difficulties. As with other skills, it is essential to focus on the students' strengths and determine the skills and methods that will be most functional for the students in the future.

Along with the use of an alternative writing instrument, strategies that have been found to support writing activities for students with ASD include:

- Fill-in-the–blanks and cloze exercises
- Multiple-choice answers to questions (e.g., students point to the correct answer)
- Scribing
- Exemplars (e.g., samples of work that demonstrate the expectations of the task)
- Reduction in the length or number of written responses
- Division of written tasks into manageable components that focus on one section at a time

- Visuals or graphic organizers to support the written task (e.g., pictures of the sequence of a story)
- Word bank of key vocabulary or frequently used words
- Rubric for task completion that specifies the essential components of a task in a clearly outlined format

When tasks are clarified and accommodated or modified as necessary, many students with ASD are more able to participate.

Mathematics

For many students with ASD, participation in mathematics can be a challenging aspect of the academic curriculum. There are several reasons for this:

- Although many mathematical concepts can be demonstrated through visual examples, they are often accompanied by sophisticated verbal instruction.
- The language of mathematics instruction has its own vocabulary, and the precision of instruction and usage of terms can vary from one instructor to another.
- Mathematical terminology can be very complex and is challenging for students who struggle with processing the language of everyday interactions.

- Along with the verbal, orthographic, and representational expressions of number, there is also the symbolic representation in the form of numerals.
- Mathematical operations are usually performed with a pencil. Many students with ASD have fine motor difficulties and learning to form numerals and manipulate them on paper may be challenging.

Students with ASD will probably be more able to comprehend and participate in activities that involve mathematics if they have developed an understanding and ability to:

- match according to various criteria (e.g., shape, type of object, colour);
- sort or separate objects by predetermined criteria (e.g., colour, shape), working towards independently determining criteria;
- pattern through ongoing use of concrete materials, sounds, lines, and so on to copy, extend, and create increasingly complex patterns.

These are some important strategies for building comprehension and enabling participation in mathematics:

- Isolate and illustrate a simple, clear visual example of each mathematical concept. Collect these in a binder so that the student can review them regularly.
- Create a personal dictionary of mathematical terms for the student. It is important for students to know how to read and speak the language of mathematical processes.
- If necessary, break up the instructional period into several discrete segments. Some students with ASD may not be able to sustain their attention on one concept for the length of an instructional period. Breaking up the instructional period also facilitates ongoing review and reinforcement of other aspects or strands of mathematics.

- Use a variety of manipulative materials as an ongoing component of instruction to enable students to generalize concepts across materials.
- If a student has ongoing difficulty with printing numerals, provide an alternative. Using number stamps or performing operations on the computer can enable a student to participate more effectively.
- As many students enjoy using the computer, whenever possible or appropriate access mathematical software that provides visuals that clearly explain and demonstrate concepts.
- Provide opportunities for allowing the student to respond using a multiple-choice format. Pointing to the correct answer may allow increased accuracy of response.

As students enter the higher grades, many have significant difficulty with showing and explaining the steps of their work. Many students with ASD are able to solve equations very quickly and write down the answer without showing all the intermediary steps of how they reached it. This may reflect the inherent fine motor difficulty experienced by the student, as well as the student's lack of internal language to solve the problem.

Some students may have difficulty verbally explaining how an answer was reached. This reflects the language processing aspect of ASD. When this happens, it will be important to determine what the expectations for the student will be and how the student's difficulties will be accommodated. It may be necessary to apply a different or modified rubric for assessment.

While some students with ASD are able to participate in some of the strands in mathematics at grade level, many will require significant accommodations or modifications to their programs. Decisions will have to be made regarding the essential components of their ongoing program and participation in mathematics.

As a student comes to each new grade, it is essential to perform an inventory of the student's skills and carefully review the previous year's IEP. Information from the plan, as well as a skill inventory, can form the basis of the student's program. However, it must be noted that if a particular skill area has been worked on for years with little success, the student may not be ready or able to grasp those concepts. It may be more important to focus on other areas that might have more relevance to the student's experience and functional abilities. For example, it may be more functional and possible for the student to learn to use a calculator rather than to recite multiplication facts.

Homework

Many students with ASD have challenges completing homework assignments, particularly as they enter the higher grades where expectations are more sophisticated and complex. There are several reasons for this:
• Many students cannot generalize between environments. What the students are able to do at school in a particular set

of circumstances, they may not be able to do in the home environment.

- Even with written reminders about task expectations, students may forget or be confused about what they are to do.
- Parents' language of instruction may be different from that of the teacher. This can cause extreme difficulty both for the parents and the student.
- It may take a student much longer to complete tasks at home because of distractions in the environment and a desire to be doing other things.
- By the end of the school day, many students are exhausted from the energy that they have had to expend to maintain their attention, regulate their behaviour, and participate in tasks. They may not have sufficient energy or attention to be able to continue task engagement through the evening.

While it can be helpful for students to have some homework, this is an issue that must be carefully discussed by the teacher and the family. An important goal is for students to be able to generalize skills between home and school. However, the *quality of family life* is very important and homework should not be the overriding feature of a family's evening.

These are some strategies for positive homework experiences:

- Reduce the number of questions to be answered.
- Change the writing expectation (e.g., shorter answers, computer-generated responses).
- Watch a story video.
- Watch a task sequence presented through video-modelling/demonstration.

- Listen to a story.
- Draw a picture (if appropriate).
- Play games such as cards (to reinforce mathematics and social skills).
- Provide students with opportunities for homework assistance at school.

social

Working together, parents and teachers can find the best approach to the nature and amount of homework to be done. *Balance* is key.

3 | COMMUNICATION AND BEHAVIOUR

Developing communication, social skills, and appropriate behaviours is an important part of the teaching and learning process. Every student is different and has unique needs.

IN THIS CHAPTER

Behaviour Management

Managing Challenging Behaviour	70
Successful Practices for Behaviour Management	72

Communication

Communication Challenges Associated with ASD	79
Strategies to Develop and Enhance Communication Skills	81

Social Skills

The Development of Social Skills for Students with ASD	89
The Fundamentals of Social Skill Instruction	93
Strategies to Facilitate Social Understanding	98

About Asperger's Disorder

Challenges Associated with Asperger's Disorder	102
Strategies to Develop and Enhance Student Skills	106

Behaviour Management

Managing Challenging Behaviour

Impairments in communication and social skills are among the primary characteristics of ASD. These skills, in turn, are intertwined with behaviour. Severe problem behaviours that some students display – such as tantrums, aggression, destructiveness, and self-injurious behaviours – may be related to the difficulties they have with communication, adapting to change, understanding social situations, and their level of functioning. The communication, social, emotional, and behavioural difficulties experienced by students with ASD can vary. In order to learn effectively and engage successfully in the life of the classroom, some students may need behavioural supports due to medical, emotional, physical, or cognitive challenges, as well perceptual or sensory differences.

Everything a student does is behaviour. Some behaviour is effective. It meets the student's need, is understood and considered appropriate by others, and reflects the student's interaction with the environment. Other behaviours may be ineffective but occur because they are a student's best available strategy for interacting with the environment and having his or her needs met.

Many of the challenging behaviours exhibited by students with ASD are methods used by the child to:
- gain something (e.g., desired object, attention);
- make a change in the environment (e.g., increase stimulation level, change to a more preferred activity);
- escape the environment (e.g., leave situation that is stressful).

Effectively managing behaviours requires that we consider not just the behaviour itself – what the student is doing – but also the underlying purpose of the behaviour. If we focus only on what the student is doing, and try to eliminate the behaviour, we may find that another behaviour arises in its place, because the underlying need has not been met. It is important to remember that inappropriate behaviours are usually in response to something in the

Behaviours have a communicative function. Managing the behaviour of students with ASD requires that we recognize and address the message behind the behaviour.

student's environment and are an attempt to communicate a need, rather than deliberate acts of aggression or purposefully negative behaviour.

Managing the behaviours of some students with ASD can be a challenging and stressful issue faced by school staff and parents. Behaviours such as destruction of property, physical aggression, self-injury, and tantrums are affected by, and can affect, the development of appropriate social and educational skills. Students exhibiting these behaviours are often at risk for exclusion and isolation (National Research Council, 2001).

Variable factors, such as those described below, may influence decisions about developing effective management strategies.

1. Definitions of problem behaviour are variable

What can be identified as a behaviour problem may change depending on the variables. For example, the student, teacher, and environment all play a significant part in whether the behaviour is acceptable. Adults often approach the subject of behaviour from the perspective of their own life experiences and current circumstances. These perspectives affect the acceptance, tolerance, internal rules, and overall framework for expectations of the student. As a result, everyone involved is likely to see the situation in a different way, on the basis of factors such as the following:
• personal childhood experiences
• cultural background
• school policies
• the individual's relationship with the student

2. Behaviour is student and situation dependent

It is often challenging to determine how the unique needs of the student should be considered in relation to expectations about the student's behaviour. For example, the expectations and response regarding a student who is unaware of the inappro-priateness of a specific behaviour would be different from those regarding a student who is aware. Likewise, factors such as the age of the student and behaviours of the student in other situations or settings come to bear on our decisions about what is considered acceptable behaviour.

Successful Practices for Behaviour Management

Managing Challenging Behaviours Is a Process

Managing challenging behaviours of students with ASD requires a collaborative team problem-solving process that includes parents and others who interact with the student. It is critical that the team consider the student's behaviour across various situations, and how to manage behaviours that arise in different settings and circumstances during the day. It is also important to establish consistency across the collaborative team, in regard to both expectations and planned responses.

One example of an effective behavioural support strategy is to help a student learn to use an alternative way to communicate feelings that have led to behaviour problems in the past. Teaching the student to use specific words, gestures, or visual supports (such as pictures) to identify and communicate feelings provides an alternative that may reduce or replace the disruptive behaviour. Behavioural support strategies help to prevent problems from occurring and enable students to acquire more effective, appropriate ways for interacting with the environment.

The principles and strategies of ABA, as discussed previously in this guide, provide an effective approach to managing the challenging behaviours of students with ASD. The focus is on measuring and tracking behaviours over time to determine the function of the target behaviour (for the student), and altering the behaviour (either increasing or decreasing its occurrence) by providing intervention.

Behaviour support plans need to be developed to manage some challenging behaviours. An effective support plan will:

- be based on a functional assessment and analysis of the student's behaviour;
- focus on the individual student;
- include methods for teaching alternatives to the behaviour problems;
- include strategies for making changes to the environmental and instructional circumstances found to be most associated with the problem.

Effective behaviour management is an ongoing process with definable steps. It begins with a functional behaviour assessment (FBA), which is a systematic process designed to look beyond the student's behaviour and focus on identifying its function or purpose. Based on the FBA, a behavioural support plan is developed to identify alternative behaviours for the student, and strategies for reducing or replacing ineffective behaviours. Finally, ongoing monitoring is used to review progress and identify any changes that need to be made.

Completing an FBA

Step 1: Define targeted behaviours

Information needs to be collected to clearly identify and describe the problematic and challenging behaviours. Collecting data about a student's behaviours helps to determine how frequently a targeted behaviour occurs and any changes that may take place over time. A variety of data-gathering methods should be considered, to ensure that a broad picture of the behaviour has been developed and that behaviours have been accurately observed, measured, and recorded.

Background information about the student can be gathered through interviews with the student, parents, teachers, or others who interact with the student, and provides valuable information about the student's patterns of behaviour both in the classroom and in other situations and circumstances. Background information can also include current and previous student information found in the student's OSR, such as the student's academic history and assessment results.

See Chapter 4:
47. Behavioural Assessments
48. Behaviour Tracking Sheet
49. Behaviour Frequency
*   Checklist*

Data can be collected indirectly, through interviews or reviewing past records, and directly, through observation. Collecting data about a particular behaviour will provide important information, including the following:

- where it happens (and does not happen)
- when it happens (and does not happen)
- who is usually present when behaviour happens (or does not happen)
- how often it happens and how long it lasts
- what else is happening in the environment
- the student's reaction to the consequences of behaviour

Observation is an effective tool for gathering information about behaviour. Ideally the student should be observed across a broad range of situations and settings, including both structured and unstructured settings. Observations can be recorded anecdotally, or using a structured data-collection method such as graphs or scatter plots. Data-collection charts, such as the following example, can be designed to track specific behaviours and situations and to identify possible factors such as time of day or activities that might influence the student's behaviour.

	Period 1	**Period 2**	**Lunchtime**	**Period 3**	**Period 4**
Behaviour A	✓✓✓✓✓	✓✓	✓	✓✓✓✓	✓✓✓ ✓✓✓
Behaviour B	✓✓✓	✓✓✓✓	✓✓	✓✓✓	✓✓✓✓ ✓✓✓

It can be useful to develop scales for tracking the intensity of a behaviour. Scales can be used to compare the perceptions of others about the behaviour, and to track changes over time. A typical scale might consist of:

- **1** = Mild disruption to others sitting nearby
- **3** = Moderate disruption to others within classroom
- **5** = Severe disruption to other classes

See Chapter 4:
50. ABC Chart
51. ABC Analysis

It is important to identify environmental factors that influence or increase the probability that the challenging behaviour will occur. A data-collection method such as ABC (Antecedent – Behaviour – Consequence) helps to determine patterns of behaviour and to identify factors that might be used to predict behaviours of concern.

ABC is a simple but effective method used to collect information about a student's behaviours. ABC tracking assists in thinking about what is happening and looking at the behaviour in the context of the whole event, not just the specific action. Through the ABC method a chart similar to the one below is used to record:

- **Antecedent:** what happens before the behaviour problem occurs
- **Behaviour:** what the student does
- **Consequence:** what happens after or as a result of the behaviour.

Antecedent	Behaviour	Consequence
(11:00) John was sitting with peers on carpet in library looking at book. The teacher directed the class to put away books and take out math activities.	John looked at the teacher and then threw the book at peer.	John was directed to leave the classroom and escorted to a chair outside the principal's office.
(11:15) John entered the classroom while students were working on math activities.	John took box of math activities from table and threw on the floor.	John was directed to leave the classroom and escorted back to the principal's office.

The ABC method can be used to track and compare information about the patterns and relationships that may have developed between a student's behaviours and other factors, such as various activities, time periods, and settings. It can be a helpful tool to identify the factors that have an effect on the behaviour, such as environmental factors and those internal to the student. For example, behaviours that occur when a student is hungry or in a crowded setting can be documented to identify whether these factors have an effect on the student's behaviour. The information in the above sample ABC chart helps to identify the possibilities that John's behaviours may be related to a desire to avoid the math activities and that an unintended reinforcement may be provided by a trip to the principal's office.

Step 2: Analyse data to develop a hypothesis about the function of the behaviour

Once data have been collected, the next step is to analyse all of the information to determine what may be causing the student to maintain the challenging behaviour, and the purpose or "function" of the behaviour. For the previous example of John, it will be necessary to consider the background information that has been gathered from various sources about John and his behaviours, as well as further observations that have been recorded about his current behaviours across various time periods and activities.

See Chapter 4:
52. Functions of Behaviour

Questions such as the following should be considered in analysing information about a student's behaviours:
- What is the behaviour of concern? Is it a new or unusual behaviour for the student?
- How frequently does this behaviour occur?
- Is there a pattern to when it occurs (e.g., time of day, activity, setting, audience)?
- What happens just before the behaviour?
- What happens following the behaviour? Is there a consistent response from others or a consequence to the behaviour?
- What is the student's reaction to the response or consequence to the behaviour? Does the behaviour change (e.g., frequency or intensity)?
- What are possibilities for the function of the behaviour for the student (e.g., gain or escape something)?

It is useful to look systematically at and analyse all of the information that has been collected to develop a hypothesis statement about the function of the student's behaviour. The hypothesis needs to be articulated as a clear statement that contains the following elements:

When [antecedent happens] the student will [inappropriate action] for the purpose of [what is gained or escaped]. This is more likely to happen if [other triggers …].

*A Sample
Hypothesis
Statement*

*When John is presented
with math activities, he
will throw items for the
purpose of escaping from
the task. This is more
likely to happen if it is
near lunchtime.*

*See Chapter 4:
53. Positive Behavioural
Intervention Plan*

Step 3: Do a functional analysis to test the hypothesis

A functional analysis is a systematic process through which antecedents and consequences are altered to develop or confirm the hypothesis about the function of the behaviour. For example, in the above case of John, we could begin a systematic process to try the following to test the hypothesis about John's behaviours:

- Provide John with other types of activities during this period.
- Introduce math activities at an earlier time in the morning or just after lunch.
- Schedule a break or walk in the hall for John prior to beginning math activities.
- Vary the types and difficulty levels of the math activities.
- Expect John to stay in the classroom and work on the task, if he throws something in response to math activities.

Through varying the antecedents and consequences, it may be found that the original hypothesis about the student's behaviour needs to be changed. For example, if John continues to throw items when other activities are presented during this period, the hypothesis statement could eventually be refined to this:

When John is presented with activities that involve group work, he will throw items for the purpose of escaping from the task. This is more likely to happen if it is near lunchtime.

Step 4: Develop a behaviour support plan

Once a hypothesis about the purpose of a behaviour is developed, a behaviour support plan can be designed to address the challenging behaviour of the student, on the basis of the earlier observation and analysis. The behaviour support plan should be individualized to the student and clearly set out what will be done to reduce the inappropriate behaviour.

The behaviour support plan is designed to:

- target the underlying reason for the behaviour;
- replace the inappropriate behaviour with an appropriate behaviour that serves the same function;
- reduce or eliminate challenging behaviour.

To develop a behaviour support plan:

- Consider how the antecedents (or environment) could be changed. For example, if the hypothesis is that the student's behaviour is due to sensory stimulation, such as excessive noise, the strategy might be to reduce the noise level.
- Identify alternative behaviours that the student can use to achieve the same purpose. For example, in the case above, John could be shown how to use a phrase or visually communicate the message that he did not want to work in the group situation, rather than throw items.
- Consider strategies and supports that may be needed to help students to learn and use alternative behaviours.

- Focus on positive reinforcement methods to identify the consequences or reinforcements that will be used.
- Use the student's strengths and interests to motivate the student.
- To help students learn to generalize appropriate skills, plan to promote the use of alternative behaviours across different settings and as independently as possible.
- Identify clearly the tasks involved and those responsible. For example, outline who will teach the student replacement behaviours, who will provide the reinforcement, and when and where the actions will take place.

It is important to remember that behaviour is established and develops over time, and that managing and changing behaviour is a process that takes time.

Step 5: Monitor progress and identify alternative strategies
It is necessary to continue monitoring the effectiveness of the interventions and behaviour support plan, and to establish a process for ongoing review and data collection to determine whether effective changes are occurring.

During this process, decisions may be made to:
- continue the current plan;
- change the plan and use alternative strategies;
- increase or decrease the degree of student support;
- target another behaviour;
- change reinforcements.

Communication

Communication Challenges Associated with ASD

The communication skills of students with ASD vary significantly. Communication challenges are central to ASD, however, and many students with ASD have difficulty communicating with others in a meaningful way or using functional communication skills.

Some students develop highly sophisticated vocabulary, although they may have difficulty using language in a way that is considered socially appropriate. Others are non-verbal and need to use an alternative form of communication, such as visuals or gestures, to share information with others. Some students do not have a method of communication that is easily recognized by others. It is important to understand the communication system that individual students use.

At least one-third of all individuals with ASD fail to develop spoken language (Bryson, 1996). Other students develop a limited vocabulary or acquire spoken language but have difficulty using language in a functional way. When speech does develop, unusual grammatical structures, pitch, tone, and inflection are common. Many students with ASD have difficulty understanding higher level, figurative language such as idioms, figures of speech, and abstract concepts. In these cases, a phrase such as "It's raining cats and dogs" is likely to be interpreted literally and misunderstood.

Non-verbal communication skills include the use of gestures, visuals, facial expressions, and body language in communications with others. These skills are often difficult for students with ASD to recognize, understand, and use.

Social communication skills are typically an area of difficulty for students with ASD. Social communication skills involve the

social initiation

interpretation and use of verbal and non-verbal communications in social situations and include skills such as initiating or sustaining conversations with others, turn taking, understanding physical proximity, and knowing how or when comments are socially appropriate.

Many students with ASD have difficulties using and understanding both verbal and non-verbal communication methods. Their communications with others may be further affected by impairments in social communication skills.

Sometimes, the communication methods used by students with ASD are unusual or not commonly used by others. As a result, their intended messages may not be understood. For example, some students frequently use made-up phrases or words that are meaningful to the student but unknown to the listener. Other students may use eye gaze or proximity to communicate a message that is not recognized or is overlooked by others.

Communication skills can significantly affect and be affected by sensitivities or impairments in other skill areas. For example, making eye contact with others during conversations and using eye gaze appropriately are common difficulties for individuals with ASD. Often, a difficulty with making eye contact is connected to a sensitivity to visual stimuli that is overwhelming to the individual.

The development and use of communication skills are closely connected to students' behaviour and social skills. Some students use unusual or socially inappropriate behaviours to communicate. Often, the message that the student is trying to communicate is not recognized as a communication attempt, or is misunderstood.

TIPS FOR TEACHERS

It is important to determine the underlying cause for a student's communication difficulties. For example, it is possible that a student who is not attentive or does not respond to communication attempts by others:

- Has difficulty processing verbal information
- Does not understand the communication method being used
- Has heard and understood the information but is unable to respond to it.

A comprehensive assessment by a speech-language pathologist (SLP) will help to determine whether the difficulty this student has in responding to information from others is due to a receptive language, processing, attention, or other difficulty.

Strategies to Develop and Enhance Communication Skills

Effective communication programs for students with ASD need to support the development of functional communication skills to enhance or increase interactions with others. A communication program should use a variety of methods that are based on the student's individual strengths and needs and the communication goals that are determined to be appropriate for the student. Decisions about the communication system that is considered most effective for a student to use are determined by an assessment of the student's current communication abilities.

peer/social methods?

The student's expressive, receptive, and social communication skills are usually assessed by an SLP. It is essential that the program to develop communication skills is at the level of the student's cognitive and linguistic development and includes methods, words, or concepts that are meaningful and functional to the child.

For students who use spoken language, the goals of a communication program could be to enhance the development of language and communication skills and to increase the use of verbal behaviours. Communication goals for students who do not use spoken language could include learning to vocalize, gesture, sign manually, or use alternative methods, such as pictures or objects, to enhance communication attempts.

Students with ASD often require direct instruction, as well as opportunities for social interactions in which to learn, develop, and practise communication skills. It is often necessary to teach the student the verbal language and other communication methods that are required across a variety of communicative situations, such as the following:

social interaction

- greetings ("Hello", wave hand)
- requests ("Please help", manual sign)
- refusals ("No, thank you", shake head)
- comments ("I live on Main Street", point to visual address).

Speech, language, and communication skills that are taught in the student's natural environment are more likely to generalize to

See Chapter 4:
54. *Communication Observation Form*
55. *Checklist for Communication Skills*
56. *Communicative Functions Observation Sheet*

TOOLS & TECHNIQUES

peers

other environments. Structured formal and informal opportunities for the student to communicate with various individuals (peers and adults) throughout the student's day will increase the possibility that the student will use the communication in other settings.

peers?

The following strategies have been found to be effective to increase communication attempts for verbal and non-verbal students with ASD in the classroom.

Communication Strategies	Examples
Reinforce that communication is a method of interacting with others by responding to students' communication attempts. It is important to be aware of and respond to a student's early attempts to communicate, such as gestures and signals involving eye gaze and proximity. Allowing a student to have access to objects or activities in which an interest has been expressed will reinforce and increase communication attempts.	Hand a student who is learning to use gestures a favourite book after the student points to the bookshelf.
Structure the learning environment so that the student needs to communicate to access objects of interest and preferred activities. Incorporating preferred items into the student's classroom will help to establish an environment in which the student is motivated to communicate in the actual setting in which similar, future communications are likely to occur.	Place a favourite item on a shelf outside of the student's reach to provide an opportunity for the student to learn to ask for assistance.
Model more effective methods of communication to increase and expand the student's communication efforts.	Model how to use the phrase "This is hard" to the student who throws a book on the floor when a task is difficult.
Provide verbal, physical, or visual prompts as signals to encourage or enhance communications. Prompts can help students who don't know what to say during routine or novel situations.	Provide a card with a written cue for an appropriate response (e.g., "It is snowing") during routine weather activity.
Pause frequently during activities the student prefers. The student's motivation to participate in or continue with a motivating activity will provide an incentive for the student to communicate.	Pause in the middle of reading a familiar part of the student's favourite story.

TIPS FOR TEACHERS

Recognizing Behaviours as Methods of Communication

Behaviours are part of the communication system and are often used to indicate information about a student's internal state or as a response to the environment (Heflin & Alaimo, 2007). The behaviours that a student with ASD uses to communicate information will be affected by impairments that the student may have in communication, behaviour, and social skill development. For example, a student may destroy materials that are difficult to understand or may hit out at others when in an uncomfortable situation or feeling tired. Teaching communication skills that are socially appropriate can help to reduce disruptive behaviours and increase social interactions. *[handwritten: social interaction]*

Helping students to develop appropriate functional communication methods has been found to reduce problem behaviours while increasing communication skills (Durand & Merges, 2001; Buckley & Newchok, 2004).

Functional communication skill development begins with an assessment and analysis of the student's behaviours to determine the intended message of the behaviour. The student is then taught replacement communication methods that are more acceptable to communicate the same message. Depending on the situation and student, the replacement functional communication methods can be verbal or non-verbal. Verbal methods involve teaching a specific phrase (e.g., "This is hard," "I need to leave"); non-verbal methods include teaching the use of pictures, gestures, or a speech-generating device. For example, the student who hits out when in an uncomfortable situation can be taught the phrase "I need to leave" or provided with a picture that will visually demonstrate to others that the student is upset and needs to leave the situation.

An important component of developing functional communication methods to replace behaviours is that the student must consistently meet with success when learning the replacement communication. Otherwise, the student may revert to the original behaviours that had previously achieved the desired results. For example, if a student is learning to use the phrase "I need to leave" to replace hitting out at others, it is important that he is consistently provided with an opportunity to leave the situation in response to the phrase.

Augmentative and Alternative Communication Methods

Augmentative and Alternative Communication (AAC) makes use of services and devices, such as visual symbols, signs, or voice output devices, to supplement (augment) or replace (serve as an alternative to) a student's current method of communication. Although AAC methods have been found to be most useful for students who do not develop functional speech or those who have difficulty processing spoken language, they are also used successfully to help verbal students to communicate or understand complex or abstract information more effectively.

There is a variety of AAC systems. They can be simply made, inexpensive, low-tech devices such as pictures and word cards. Others can also be more complex, expensive, high-tech systems such as computerized voice output devices with synthesized and digitized speech. In many cases, AAC systems are portable and can be used in different settings. They are reasonably easy for others to understand and use.

Visual systems use communication boards, objects, picture cards, or visual symbols to support or expand spontaneous, functional communication attempts for some students with ASD. In most cases, the visuals are organized thematically in a system that is easy for the student to access across various settings.

The use of visuals to support communication is most effective when:

- Visuals **reflect the student's particular interests** or needs
- Students take an **active role** in using and handling visual materials
- Students **establish a connection** between the activity or object and the visual
- Visual systems are **readily available** (e.g., kept in a consistent location) to the students and others in the environment
- Visuals are **durable** and quickly replaceable
- Visual systems are **used consistently**.

Echolalia

Echolalia is the repetition of the words or phrases used by others. It can be immediate (occur right after the original utterances) or delayed (occur significantly later than them). Echolalia is common in students with ASD and has been found to serve a variety of purposes. In some situations and for some students, echolalia is used as a method to communicate or interact with others or in response to something in the student's environment. In other cases, echolalia has no apparent communicative or interactive function and appears to be a form of practice for the student to learn language or regulate self-behaviour. The use of echolalia increases when some students have difficulty comprehending language. Regardless of the type or purpose of echolalia, it should be considered as part of the child's system of communication, rather than an isolated behaviour (Rydell & Prizant, 1995).

It is important not to assume that the student understands or is intentionally using the content of the echolalic speech being used. For example, a student may repeat a phrase in response to a situation that is causing anxiety. The phrase that is used by the student to indicate anxiety may not be related to specific details in the current situation, but is a phrase that was used in a previous stressful situation. In this case, teaching the student to recognize anxious feelings, practise calming techniques, and use an alternative phrase such as "I'm upset" to indicate anxiety may be an appropriate intervention.

An assessment and analysis of the student's echolalic behaviours and patterns within the context of the student's environment should be done to understand the role and purpose of the echolalia and to determine the interventions that will be effective for the student. Individualized goals and strategies should be developed according to an analysis of the student's use of echolalia. The goal of strategies could be to expand, reduce, or replace the echoic utterances.

TIPS FOR TEACHERS

EXAMPLES OF INTERVENTION METHODS

Goal	Intervention Examples
To *expand* echoic utterances that are considered early communicative attempts	• Acknowledge and appropriately respond to communication attempt • Model expanded phrase
To *reduce* inappropriate echolalia that is caused by situations that are stressful to the student	• Modify environment that has been found to cause stress for student • Teach student strategies to reduce feelings of stress (e.g., relaxation techniques)
To *replace* echolalia that is considered inappropriate	• Model alternative phrase • Provide AAC such as a visual for student to use as an alternative

TOOLS & TECHNIQUES

*See Chapter 4:
57. Answering the
Telephone*

peers?

Enhancing Communications with Students

The possibility of successful communications can be increased by being aware of and using strategies such as the following to enhance and support communications with students:

• Communicate at the student's level.
• Establish the student's attention.
• Prepare the student for what is going to be communicated.
• Support messages visually with gestures, body language, and pictures.
• Speak slowly and clearly.
• Don't overload the student with information.
• Pause to allow the student time to comprehend and respond.
• Guide or prompt the student to respond if needed.
• Stay with the interaction or repeat until the desired response is achieved.

(Hodgdon, 1999)

Social Skills

The Development of Social Skills for Students with ASD

When considering the development of social interaction skills for students with ASD, it is important to keep in mind that impairment in the area of social skills is associated with a diagnosis of the disorder. Individuals with ASD generally do not learn social skills through incidental experiences and exposure to social situations. Most often, it is necessary to work on skill development by directly teaching the language and rituals of social interaction. Students with ASD also need to be provided opportunities to use their social skills and generalize them to the larger school environment, home, and community.

Building a Foundation for Skill Development

When a student with ASD enters school, it is important for the teacher, support personnel, and parents to discuss and develop a comprehensive profile of the social skills already used by the student in other environments, such as the preschool, daycare, home, and community settings. It is necessary to observe the student in the school setting to see how or whether these skills are generalizing to the new school environment. When an accurate picture has been formed, a plan for social skill development can be devised.

It is important for both teachers and parents to keep in mind that the development of social interaction skills will take time, patience, and consistency. There is a continuum of development from fundamental skills, such as learning to share toys, to the complex issues of adolescence and young adulthood. Skill development may come quickly at some points and slowly at others, depending on the student's ability to receive information and the intensity of focus in other skill areas.

TOOLS & TECHNIQUES

See Chapter 4:
58. Social Interaction

How Peers Can Help

An important component in building a solid foundation for skill development is the creation of a climate in the classroom and school in which individual differences are understood, accepted, and accommodated. Peers will play a significant role in helping a student learn how to interact successfully.

While many natural social interactions between the student with ASD and his classmates will occur in the daily round of school activities, sometimes a more formalized arrangement is required to promote interactions. Peers can take on the roles of being supportive buddies during recess and lunch, in the library and gym, at the computer, and during cooperative work periods for specific subjects.

Guidelines for Buddy Systems

- Explain to the group the purpose of being a buddy: to help their classmate learn to have friends and develop social skills.
- Participation must be voluntary. Occasionally a classmate initially may not wish to be a buddy.
- Give some ownership of the process to the class. Allow the class to generate ideas for activities and ways to help their classmate.
- Arrange for buddies to work in pairs so that they can talk about and plan their activities.

Also, when there are two buddies, should an incident occur on the schoolyard, for instance, one student can stay with the classmate, while the other seeks assistance.

- As in the case of any individual, the student with ASD may, at times, wish to be alone. This must be acknowledged, as sometimes students feel overwhelmed and need quiet times to "regroup" so that they can move forward in their day calmly.

While the student with ASD may benefit from both formal and informal interactions with classmates and other students in the school, others will also benefit from their association with the student with ASD by developing an understanding and appreciation of human difference.

Peer Awareness

Most students are curious about the nature of a classmate's difference. When this happens, it may be helpful to create a level of awareness about ASD. Demystification of disability opens the

awareness
understanding
acceptance

door to communication and understanding of individual strengths and abilities. With understanding comes acceptance. This, however, raises some important considerations:

- Caution must always be used to protect the right to privacy of the student and the family. Any disclosure of information must be done in a manner consistent with school board policies and applicable privacy legislation.

- If the student's parents want information about their child's diagnosis or characteristics to be shared with classmates and other people in the school, it is important to discuss how it should be shared. Some parents will choose to come into the class and explain the nature of the diagnosis and how it is manifested in their child, while others will prefer that the teacher share this information and perhaps distribute an appropriate piece of children's literature on disability and difference. (See the list of children's books on ASD in Appendix B: Resources).

- It is necessary to consider whether the student with ASD is aware of the diagnosis and the student's level of comfort with this information being shared with classmates. In some cases, students with ASD have been the ones to share the information (giving them control of the process).

- Parents and teachers need to decide whether the student with ASD should be present during the sharing session. Sometimes, classmates are more comfortable asking their questions if the student is not present. In other situations, the student with ASD may be able to answer classmates' questions and participate in the experience.

- In all cases, whether specific information about a student can be shared or not, it is important that a comfort level for all students be established. Opportunities for students to recognize and appreciate aspects of human difference, such as individual strengths and abilities, should be an ongoing part of instruction. There is also a growing body of children's literature dealing with disability and difference, which can serve to open discussion and facilitate learning. In a multicultural, inclusive society, it is crucial that students be prepared to understand and accept human difference in all of its forms.

Social
construction
model
of disability

peers?

The Issue of Eye Contact

The establishment and maintenance of eye contact is often regarded as one of the fundamental components of social interaction. However, many individuals with ASD report that they can either look at others or listen to others, but not do both. Making eye contact is a factor that frequently compounds their difficulties with social interaction.

In some cases, it is appropriate to work towards building eye contact during social interaction, if only for short periods. As eye contact during social interaction is valued in our society, encouragement and training for play and social interaction may be the most appropriate starting point. Work slowly and carefully. Generally, as a student gets to know you and becomes accustomed to the sound of your voice, he or she will be more likely to look at you comfortably.

A reasoned and moderate approach to this issue will help to alleviate anxiety for a student who, with time, may become more able to establish eye contact. It is critical to keep in mind that this will be to the student's comfort level, not to ours.

Some individuals with ASD will continue to have difficulties with making eye contact. Their communications with others are easier when they focus on another physical detail of the speaker or in the environment. It is important to consider that emphasizing or focusing on the skill of making eye contact may reduce or limit the student's abilities to communicate.

"How much easier it is to hear someone if you can't see his or her face. Then words are pure and not distorted by grimaces and gestures. I can listen better to the tone of someone's voice when I am not confused by the unwritten words of their facial expressions."
(Lawson, 1998: 97)

Theory of Mind

Simply described, "Theory of Mind" is the ability to attribute thoughts and feelings to others. Individuals with ASD generally have difficulty imagining how other people may be feeling in a situation or forming hypotheses about what others may be thinking. Because of this, understanding the nuances of social interaction may be very difficult.

Students with ASD are often unable to discern unwritten social rules and may find themselves in social difficulty because of their inability to perceive the subtleties of interaction. Very often, direct teaching and ongoing mentoring are necessary to help the student develop an awareness of expectations and to generalize appropriate responses and behaviours across the school environment.

peers?

Although it is difficult for many students with ASD to develop a comprehensive understanding of what other people may be thinking or feeling, such students can be provided with the tools needed to manage their social behaviours and establish relationships with others to the best of their ability.

The Fundamentals of Social Skill Instruction

To facilitate positive interactions at school, the following social skills are particularly important for students to learn:
- greetings √
- initiating and closing interactions √
- choosing activities √
- sharing √
- waiting X
- turn taking X
- playing games √

6/8 peers reforored

Greetings

When teaching students with ASD how to greet others, observe how other students in the class and at that age level greet each other. While shaking hands with someone is good manners, it is rarely appropriate for peer interactions. Student with ASD may initially need to be prompted through the greeting, as well as reinforced for all efforts. Peers should also be reinforced for being partners in teaching this important skill.

peers as teachers.

Very often, school staff will greet the student as he or she travels in the halls of the school. As days are busy, they may be in a hurry or not realize that the student with ASD (as well as students with other developmental disabilities) may not be able to respond as quickly to a greeting as others can. People in the school need to know that if they greet the student, they must be prepared to wait the 10 or 20 seconds it may take the student with ASD to respond.

Initiating and Closing Interactions

Social scripts (see "Social Scripts" in the "Strategies to Facilitate Social Understanding" section below) can be a very useful strategy to help students know the expectations of how to enter a play situation or how to ask someone to play. It is important to keep in mind that this is a skill that can be difficult for many other students as well, who might also benefit from direct instruction in this area. While instructing and coaching the student with ASD on how to initiate an interaction or enter a play situation, it is also important to coach peers on how to receive the student, that is, how to be welcoming.

[handwritten margin notes: Social initiation; impact peers; peers]

TOOLS & TECHNIQUES
See Chapter 4:
59. Joining a Conversation

Similarly, students with ASD need to know how to leave a play situation politely. Through direct teaching, which might include demonstration, rehearsal, and prompting, the student is instructed through "leaving" scenarios. Peers are also coached to demonstrate a wave or to say "See you later" or another phrase denoting closure.

[handwritten margin notes: peer coaching; peers]

Choosing Activities

As previously discussed in this guide, transitions between activities are often difficult for students with ASD, and choosing a new activity can lead to increased anxiety and unusual or inappropriate behaviours. The following strategies have been found to be useful in helping students make a choice about activities:

- Clearly note "Activity Time" on the students' visual schedules.
- Provide a visual choice board using either photographs or picture symbols to inform the students of the available activities.
- Allow students to have autonomy over the choice process. In the early grades, it can be difficult for students with ASD to understand that only two or three children are allowed to be in specific centres at a time. Sometimes flexibility is key, and providing positive transition experiences might be more effective than following the rules rigidly.
- Sometimes, students have one preferred activity at which they would choose to spend all of their time. When this happens, it

is helpful to provide transition warnings, such as using a timer, to let the students know that it is time to move to another activity. Once the preferred activity has been selected, it is removed from the choice board and is no longer available as a choice. This is simple, visual, and obvious and can encourage students to broaden their interests.

• When engaging with peers, it will be important for the student with ASD to work towards being able to participate in another classmate's activity choice. This should be done with a supportive and preferred peer. Initially, this may be possible only for a short period of time, and the length of time be extended naturally or in small increments.

peers/ social interaction

Sharing

The concept of sharing is fairly abstract and, similar to Theory of Mind, involves an understanding that others have a need or desire for something and will share with us. Students with ASD often have difficulty understanding either what sharing means or why it is necessary. Sharing is a skill that may need to be taught directly.

as do many children!

• Initially, the concept of sharing may be best taught in a quiet, non-distracting environment. The instructor would have control of the materials (e.g., building blocks), which are visible to the student.

• The word "share" is emphasized with simple language as the student is handed a block (e.g., "I share the blocks.").

• This continues, with the sharing statement being repeated each time, until the student has several blocks.

• The student is then given an instruction to share. At this point, the student may need to be prompted to give a block to the instructor. This prompt may be gestural: the instructor holds out a hand and says, "Share." If the student is able to do so, praise lavishly.

peer?

• If the student is not able to follow through, then continue to repeat instructional sessions. The materials for sharing can vary across sessions.

• Important throughout is the student's awareness that he is not going to lose the item by sharing it. He, too, will be able to participate in using it.

peer

- When the concept has been learned, add a supportive peer to the situation and work on extension of the skill to include sharing with the peer.
- When the student has learned to share in a structured process, activities can be created in the classroom for the student to practise sharing in other situations, such as sharing art supplies.
- While this process may appear to be lengthy and involved, careful training for sharing can help students learn this important skill.

Waiting

Being able to wait, either to take one's turn, to eat lunch, or to go home, is a critical life skill. This is a skill that may have to be developed incrementally, using specific tools and strategies, which can include the following:

- a "First …, then …" board
- a visual schedule
- a timing device
- distracters, such as tokens that can be removed one at a time to denote a "countdown"
- a high rate of reinforcement for waiting
- reliable follow-through: the student has waited, so he receives the item

Turn Taking

Like sharing, turn taking is another skill that initially may be best taught directly in a quiet, non-distracting environment. The student needs to know what the term means and what it involves. When teaching turn taking:

- use a simple or familiar toy or game. The act of taking turns can be demonstrated for the student while he is prompted (if necessary) through the turn-taking process. Key terms, such as "My turn" and "Your turn", must be associated with the movements involved;
- reinforce the student's participation in the process of waiting for a turn;
- occasionally pause before saying "Your turn" so that the student will develop an awareness of having to wait for the verbal cue.

peers?

TOOLS & TECHNIQUES

See Chapter 4:
60. Activities to Promote Turn Taking
61. Prompts Used in Turn Taking

Playing Games

By teaching students with ASD the specific skills that they will need for various activities and games, we enable students to enter into activities with a foundation of information and skills that they can apply to situations, and to be as independent as possible.

See Chapter 4:
62. Play Checklist
63. Fitness Friends Program
64. Integrated Games Group

While many games appear to be simple, actually they are composed of fairly complicated sets of subskills. Teaching the student to play a game may be most successful when done in a quiet, non-distracting environment. These are some suggestions for teaching students with ASD to participate in games:

- In a step-by-step manner, introduce the game materials and demonstrate how to use them. Use as little language as possible. When dice are involved, it is worth the effort to help a student learn to automatically recognize the numbers represented by the dots. Otherwise the endless counting of dots will slow down the process of play when the student is with his peers.
- Demonstrate the expectations of the game (e.g., throwing a ball towards a target, moving a game piece, matching cards).
- Perform a task analysis to determine each step of the game. Incrementally demonstrate and practise the steps, adding each new step as the student experiences success.
- Practise the game regularly until the student understands the routines.
- When the student is comfortable playing with an adult, introduce a supportive peer to the game and rehearse until the student with ASD is again comfortable.
- If possible, videotape a small group of students playing the game so that the student can watch the routines and rituals of play over and over again so that he can develop an understanding of group expectations.
- Introduce the student to the group situation and step back. Let the student play as independently as possible.

By taking the time to develop the ability to play a game without constant peer or adult reminders and support, a life skill is developed. When a student is able to play independently without adult supervision and coaching, he is more likely to be included with peers. By taking this time, we are not only teaching the student

*[handwritten note: * first adults then peers. ∖ conducive to classroom ?]*

[handwritten note: video model.]

*with ASD valuable game-playing skills, but also facilitating positive social interaction. *— for both students with and without ASD!*

social participation

The acquisition of these fundamental social interaction and play skills will facilitate social relationships with peers. As well, such skills will serve as a foundation on which to build skills as the student moves on to other environments.

Strategies to Facilitate Social Understanding

TOOLS & TECHNIQUES

See Chapter 4:
65. Social Scenario
66. My Morning Routine

Social Scripts

Social interaction

For the child with ASD, the use of social scripts can play an integral role in the development of social skills. Scripts can be written to target the various situations in which a student regularly participates in order to teach what an individual should say and do in particular situations. They are used to clarify and provide a model of the language and processes of social interaction. Social scripts break down social situations into steps and clearly outline expectations, such as the rules or guidelines for social behaviour and good manners.

Tips for Composing Scripts

TIPS FOR TEACHERS

- Write a social script much like the script of a play, the words guiding the action and interaction. For example, a social script might be written on what to say when asking a peer to play a game.
- Rehearse over and over again until the student is confident about the conversational or action routine. It can then be embellished through natural, but directed, occurrence.
- Read the script with the student in various settings and at different times of day. Students need to be able to go through the conversational routine of the script without prompting; therefore, they may need to repeat particular conversations.

- Introduce the routine of the script without using the printed copy.
- Gradually add new components to the script, if possible without adding them to the printed copy. Make the new components as small as necessary. As the script is "played out" in different environments, add elements that are particular to the specific environment.
- Work for mastery of one script at a time.
- When the student is ready and a situation warrants, prepare a new script. If possible, use some of the words from previous scripts (controlled vocabulary).
- Create a "script book" in which the conversations are collected. Review them regularly.

Stories That Teach Social Understanding

Stories that are designed to teach or clarify social understanding differ from social scripts in that they explain why people act in certain ways rather than focus on the "how to" aspects of social situations. The idea is to inform the reader simply, clearly, and in a reassuring manner how and why he or she should respond in a certain way. Negative behaviours are not stated in this kind of a story, and alternative, positive behaviours are suggested. Such a story might explain how students can manage their time and behaviour at recess, and the ideal time to read this story would be before the bell signalling the beginning of recess rings.

TOOLS & TECHNIQUES

See Chapter 4:
67. Steps to Reading Body
*   Language*
68. Body and Facial
*   Expressions*

Recognizing Emotions and Facial Expressions

Questions such as the following could be used with pictures (e.g., photographs of the student, parents, siblings; picture symbols; magazine pictures) to illustrate a range of emotions:

- What does happy (sad, angry, frightened, bored, etc.) look like?
- What makes me happy? (photo of child and preferred items)
- What makes Mommy happy?
- What makes Daddy happy?
- What makes my teacher happy?

A book can be created for each of the emotions (e.g., "What Is Happy?" book). Keep in mind that this recognition and understanding will not develop quickly for many students. These books may need to travel with the student from year to year. It will be important to update and add to them as classmates and staff change.

The Use of Media in Developing Social Awareness

Popular television shows and movies can be used to teach and reinforce understanding of social situations and facial expressions. When playing a recorded program or movie, use the pause button on the remote control to stop the video at key points, and then ask questions such as:

- Is the character a boy or a girl?
- What is the character's name?
- What is he wearing?

- What expression is on his face?
- How does the character feel? Is he sad?
- Why is he sad?

A "feelings chart" containing, for example, picture symbols or photos, can be provided so that students can match and note the facial expressions of the characters.

It may be necessary to watch the video several times before students can answer the questions accurately.

Issues in Adolescence

Many fundamental social skills can be developed while students are in the primary and junior grades; however, as students enter the intermediate and secondary years, with puberty the social dynamics among peers begin to change, and peer relationships become more complex. Trying to understand interpersonal social dynamics at the intermediate and secondary levels can be a significant challenge for students with ASD. It is important to note that students with ASD may not share many of the social concerns of their classmates, such as issues of boy/girl relationships, status, fashion, and cliques.

There are, however, some areas of particular concern, such as hygiene and sexuality, for all students at this stage of development. This is a time when positive communication between home and school can serve the student well, as discussing any issues of concern is important. Issues such as body odour or inappropriate sexual behaviour must be tackled forthrightly, leaving no room for question. Students need to learn about their changing bodies, how to approach members of the opposite sex, and rules about appropriate sexual behaviour. This learning can be supported and reinforced at school and home. Methods for discussing these personal issues in ways that are dignified for the student, the family, and the school staff must be established.

See Chapter 4:
69. Different Kinds of Touch
70. Public/Private Places

Privacy

Students with ASD may need to have specific knowledge about what is private and what is public. Privacy includes knowing how to use a large, public washroom appropriately, as well as knowing what parts of their bodies are private and who may touch their body (i.e., their doctor). Definite rules need to be established and adherence to them coached and reinforced.

Privacy also concerns students' personal information – their name, address, and so on. Students need to know the persons with whom it is safe to share that information. A significantly important example of this is the use or misuse of the Internet.

Safety

Many of the issues mentioned above can affect a student's safety, both in the school and in the community. Students with disabilities can be vulnerable and may easily be victimized or bullied. It is essential that the student be given clear and definite rules about how to respond in difficult situations, for example, how to call for help. Because students with ASD have difficulty generalizing, it is important that parents and school personnel share and teach the same rules.

As students approach the last years in the school system, ongoing attention to social issues and social skill development is critically important for some students with ASD. Social skills will guide the individual's ability to form relationships, have a social life, and understand what he or she needs to do in order to be safe. These goals are usually foremost in the minds of parents as they see their child move toward adulthood. Working together in positive ways, we can give students as many tools as possible to help them manage at home, at school, and in the larger community environment.

About Asperger's Disorder

Challenges Associated with Asperger's Disorder

Asperger's Disorder, commonly known as Asperger's syndrome or Asperger's, is one of the disorders found within the range of ASDs. Some unique features related to a diagnosis of this disorder are outlined in *DSM-IV-TR* (APA, 2000), and specific strategies should be considered for students in whom this disorder has been diagnosed.

A diagnosis of Asperger's Disorder is associated with the characteristics described below.

Impairment in Skill Areas	Characteristic Behaviours
Social Skills • Severe and sustained impairment in social interaction	• Has difficulty interacting with peers and adults; typically demonstrates one-sided and eccentric social behaviours • Has difficulty reading and understanding social situations
Communication Skills • No significant general delay in language acquisition, but difficulties with more subtle aspects of social communication	• Learns words and phrases at the typical age, but displays difficulties with conversational skills (e.g., misunderstanding and misusing non-verbal communications, monopolizing conversations)
Behaviour • Restricted, repetitive, and stereotypical patterns of behaviour, interests, and activities • No significant delay, if any, in cognitive development or in the development of age-appropriate self-help skills, adaptive behaviour, and curiosity about the environment in childhood	• Displays obsessions or preoccupations with specific themes or interests, often to the exclusion of other activities • Adheres inflexibly to rules or non-functional routines • Has repetitive motor mannerisms, such as hand or finger flapping

INSIGHT

The most significant differences between students with Asperger's Disorder and those in whom another ASD is diagnosed are that these students generally are considered higher functioning in many areas and do not have clinically significant delays in the development of early language or cognitive skills. Early language skills, such as using single words and spontaneous communication phrases, are usually within normal limits and in some cases may be seen as advanced or precocious during the preschool years. Many students with Asperger's Disorder have average intellectual abilities, and they may perform as well as or better than typical students in some academic areas, especially those that involve rote memory skills such as the recall of factual information.

Although students with Asperger's Disorder typically have been found to have average or above-average cognitive skills, they often display subtle but important differences in cognitive processing abilities. These students usually have the cognitive abilities to learn information but may have difficulties in:

- *comprehending complex or abstract information;*
- *learning and using the information in the context of the social environment of schools;*
- *problem solving;*
- *generalizing knowledge and skills.*

See Chapter 4:
71. Tips for Job Coaches

However, students in whom Asperger's Disorder is diagnosed have a severe social deficit, which makes understanding and using age-appropriate social behaviours and social communication skills difficult. They often have difficulty learning social skills incidentally by watching and interacting with others, and often misunderstand social situations. These difficulties affect the development of friendships and relationships with peers and adults.

Students with Asperger's Disorder usually speak fluently and are able to use routine language for social interactions. However, difficulties are common with social communication skills such as the following:

- communicating with others (e.g., talking *at* rather than *with* others)
- using social rules of conversation (e.g., turn taking and listening to others)
- initiating and maintaining extended conversations
- changing topics in conversations
- using and understanding non-verbal communication skills (e.g., facial expressions)
- comprehending the social context or multiple meanings of language
- using common speech patterns (e.g., inflection or pitch)

Some students with Asperger's Disorder have a preoccupation and heightened interest in a specific topic of interest in which they become very knowledgeable. They are intensely motivated to gather and share a great deal of detailed information on this topic. However, the social communication difficulties of the student usually affect the student's ability to recognize or respond to the interest level of the audience with whom the information is being shared.

Usually, students in whom Asperger's Disorder is diagnosed do not have clinically significant delays in the development of age-appropriate self-help skills. However, the effects of unusual behaviours and impairments in social interaction can cause significant impairments in social, occupational, or other important areas of functioning. Motor coordination difficulties that may affect fine motor and gross motor skills, as well as organizational skills, are areas of concern for some students.

Similar to students with other disorders, students in whom Asperger's Disorder is diagnosed are a diverse group, and impairments can vary according to the individual and situations or tasks. Some students with Asperger's Disorder have the cognitive skills to successfully complete postsecondary programs and enter

KEY FACTS

Asperger's Disorder has been found to be associated with other disorders, such as Depressive Disorder or Anxiety Disorder. Many students with Asperger's Disorder have difficulty with overactivity or inattention. In them, Attention-Deficit/ Hyperactivity Disorder (ADHD) may be diagnosed before Asperger's Disorder is (APA, 2000).

the workforce as relatively independent adults. The self-sufficiency skills of others may be significantly affected by impairments in adapting to social situations. Younger students may have little or no interest in establishing friendships. Adolescents, however, may have an interest in establishing friendships but experience social isolation because of difficulties with age-appropriate reciprocal social skills.

See Chapter 4:
72. Stress Thermometer
73. Relaxation Steps
74. Study Tips for Teens

The difficulties that students with Asperger's Disorder have in academic or social situations often increase or become more obvious during adolescence. As students at this stage are expected to learn, analyse, and use more abstract and complex information, the difficulties of students with Asperger's Disorder have an increased effect on their participation in learning activities. They often become aware of their social or academic difficulties or differences, and as a result become self-conscious or anxious in social and academic situations. Some students develop a sense of social isolation in adolescence, with increased anxieties, depression, or withdrawn behaviours.

It is not unusual for the behaviours of students with Asperger's Disorder to be misinterpreted by adults and peers. For example, a student may be able to read advanced books on a topic of interest but unable to read another book at the same reading level on a topic of limited interest to the student. This may be seen as a behaviour that demonstrates deliberate task avoidance or refusal.

Because of the strengths and "normally" developing skills that students with Asperger's Disorder may have, the impairments and difficulties in social and behavioural functioning can be overlooked or misunderstood. These students often want to establish friendships or relate to others but may not have developed the appropriate skills, and their interactions or responses are perceived as being unusual. For example, in an attempt to be accurate or honest or to converse with others, a student may make an observational comment that is considered offensive or inappropriate to others. Students with Asperger's Disorder may be unaware of the impact on others of what they are saying or doing, and are at an increased risk of becoming victims of teasing and bullying by peers.

In many cases, a diagnosis of Asperger's Disorder is not made until the student is in school and impairment in the development of age-appropriate social behaviours becomes more evident. Some students with Asperger's Disorder may be in school for several years before what have been seen as unusual or odd behaviours are recognized as characteristics of a disorder.

Strategies to Develop and Enhance Student Skills

Many of the strategies that have been found effective for teaching students with ASD may also be effective for students with Asperger's Disorder. The following strategies specifically address some of the common characteristics and difficulties of students with Asperger's Disorder. It is important that the learning profile and strengths and needs of the individual student be considered in determining the strategies that will be most effective for the student.

may also be effective for ALL children

STRATEGIES FOR STUDENTS WITH ASPERGER'S DISORDER

Social Interactions

peers

TIPS FOR TEACHERS

- Provide explicit or direct teaching of social rules and skills.
- Break social situations into a sequence of steps.
- Model or script steps within social interactions.
- Provide a variety of opportunities for the student to understand, recognize, and practise social rules and skills. Examples include:
  - Establishing structured and unstructured opportunities for the student to socialize with peers (e.g., lunch program, small group outings) through a circle of friends, peer partners, or buddies
  - Planning cooperative group activities
  - Providing opportunities for the student to interact with others in a shared interest (e.g., a hobby).
- Identify for the student what is happening and why.
- Encourage the student to monitor and provide feedback about social actions of self and others.
- Use video- or audiotapes of social interactions to identify, analyse, predict, or teach specific verbal social skills (e.g., "What is he doing?" "What did he say?") and non-verbal social skills.
- Provide opportunities to generalize social skills by rehearsing across a variety of settings with various individuals, including highly structured to less structured to real-life situations (in school, home, and community).

STRATEGIES FOR STUDENTS WITH ASPERGER'S DISORDER (continued)

Social Communications

- Provide explicit teaching to help the student recognize, understand the meaning of, and use non-verbal communications (e.g., gestures, facial expressions).
- Practise using social communication skills with peers and adults.
- Provide cues and prompts (e.g., visual cues for initiating conversations, your turn/my turn cards).
- Use clear, specific language.
- Explain language that is confusing for the student, and provide examples and opportunities to learn and use language (e.g., metaphors, words with multiple meanings).
- Teach the student how to monitor his or her own understanding and request that information be repeated or clarified.
- Check with the student to determine understanding; be aware of messages that the student may find unclear or misinterpret.
- Provide opportunities for role playing and rehearsal of conversations in predicted social situations (e.g., turn taking in conversations).

Limited Range of Interests

- Provide the student with a scheduled time to engage in preferred activities.
- Provide the student with varied and meaningful opportunities to use knowledge of an area.
- Incorporate other activities gradually and prepare the student for a change in activities.
- Encourage participation in new activities by connecting new activities to an area of interest.

Motor Coordination

- Use technology to enhance written output.
- Provide structured instruction for motor tasks (e.g., how to tie shoelaces).
- Provide additional opportunities for the student to practise motor tasks.
- Provide alternatives or accommodations when possible (e.g., use fill-in-the-blank activities, provide additional time).

Anxiety

- Provide the student with a method to recognize, rate, and monitor anxiety (e.g., thermometer; rating scale; colour-coded sequence to indicate green = okay, red = not okay).
- Teach self-calming or relaxation techniques (e.g., listening to music, taking deep breaths).
- Provide scheduled opportunities as needed to make the environment less stressful (e.g., student "downtime" doing a pre-selected, calming activity).

(continued)

STRATEGIES FOR STUDENTS WITH ASPERGER'S DISORDER (continued)

Anxiety (continued)

- Be aware of and prepare the student for anxiety-causing situations (e.g., provide advance warning, teach coping strategies).
- Monitor and respond to signs of teasing or bullying from others.
- Provide the student with strategies to recognize and respond to teasing or bullying.
- Provide reassurance and positive feedback to reinforce the student's efforts and accomplishments.

Organizational Skills

- Provide training or assistance with specific, individualized strategies to help the student be organized (e.g., use input from the student to set up a coded binder system to help keep track of and organize notes).
- Build an organizational system into routines (e.g., weekly tidying of locker or desk).
- Use visual supports to organize information and materials (e.g., visual schedule, homework checklist, graphic organizer, colour- or picture-coded binder sections).

4 | TOOLS AND TECHNIQUES

Ontario educators use a wide range of strategies, tools, and resources to provide effective educational programs for students with ASD. Some of the materials that have been developed by school boards and regional autism service providers are reproduced, with permission, in chapter, and may be used by schools and school boards across the province.

IN THIS CHAPTER

1.	Online Autism Modules	112
2.	Information Pamphlet for Administrators	113
3.	Survey for Parents	115
4.	Student's Day at School	116
5.	School Communication	117
6.	Information Pamphlet on ASD	118
7.	Critical Information Sheet	120
8.	Student Profile	121
9.	Promoting Independence	123
10.	Inventory of Functional Skills	124
11.	Autism Transitional Classroom	129
12.	Think Tank on Autism	131
13.	Resources for Drivers	133
14.	Transportation Visuals	134
15.	Autism Demonstration Site	135
16.	Strategies Checklist	136
17.	Classroom Layout	137

18. Morning Routine 139
19. Safety Plan: Crisis Protocol 140
20. Information for Occasional Teachers 141
21. Suggestions to Support Transitions 142
22. Preparing Students for a Special Event 143
23. Task Sequence for Home Time 144
24. Visuals for Transition from School to Home ... 145
25. Visual Steps for Using Workout Room 146
26. Visuals for School Activities 147
27. Visuals for Going to Work 148
28. Bus Rules 149
29. Getting Ready for the Bus 150
30. Individualized Daily Schedule 151
31. Monday Schedule 152
32. Classroom/Environment 153
33. Ten Ways to Create Classroom Structure 154
34. Selecting Student Organizers 155
35. How to Prompt 156
36. Prompt Tracking Sheet 157
37. Prompts Used in Initiating Play 158
38. Following Directions 159
39. Interest Inventory 160
40. Reinforcement Inventory by Parent 161
41. Reinforcement Inventory for Elementary Student ... 163
42. Giving Praise Effectively 165
43. Reinforcer Chart 166
44. Ten Recommendations 167
45. Visual Lotto Game 169
46. Visual Sentence Strip 171
47. Behavioural Assessments 172
48. Behaviour Tracking Sheet 173
49. Behaviour Frequency Checklist 174
50. ABC Chart 175
51. ABC Analysis 176
52. Functions of Behaviour 177
53. Positive Behavioural Intervention Plan 178
54. Communication Observation Form 180
55. Checklist for Communication Skills 181
56. Communicative Functions Observation Sheet ... 183
57. Answering the Telephone 184

58. Social Interaction   185
59. Joining a Conversation   187
60. Activities to Promote Turn Taking   188
61. Prompts Used in Turn Taking   189
62. Play Checklist   190
63. Fitness Friends Program   191
64. Integrated Games Group   192
65. Social Scenario   194
66. My Morning Routine   196
67. Steps to Reading Body Language   197
68. Body and Facial Expressions   198
69. Different Kinds of Touch   199
70. Public/Private Places   200
71. Tips for Job Coaches   201
72. Stress Thermometer   202
73. Relaxation Steps   203
74. Study Tips for Teens   204

Many of the illustrations in this chapter include Picture Communication Symbols, ©1981-2007 by Mayer-Johnson LLC. All Rights Reserved Worldwide. Used with permission.

1. Online Autism Modules

An Exciting New Online Resource:

Autism Spectrum Disorders
Putting the Pieces Together

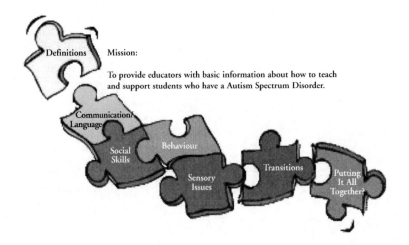

Mission:

To provide educators with basic information about how to teach and support students who have a Autism Spectrum Disorder.

The Avon Maitland District School Board provides a unique, professional learning opportunity for teachers, educational assistants, and administrators interested in acquiring more knowledge and a deeper understanding of students with Autism Spectrum Disorders.

Basic, vital information regarding the teaching and support for these children is available in a seven-module, user-friendly format.

The online modules, entitled **"Autism Spectrum Disorders: Putting the Pieces Together,"** include Definitions, Communication, Social Skills, Behaviour, Sensory Issues, Transitions and Putting It All Together.

Also offered are:
- Quick links to related websites
- A list of the "Top 10" ASD resource books
- Examples of visual communication ideas such as schedules and task strips

Access the modules at http://amdsb.mycourses.ca.

2. Information Pamphlet for Administrators

School-Based Team Meeting

A school-based team meeting is an effective method of bringing the needed players together. The parents can invite who they believe would be needed for information sharing (current personnel who work with their child). The principal invites appropriate system specialists and, if needed, their Community Care Access Centre contact.

The purpose of a school-based team meeting is to:

- Consider the plan for school transition and school start.
- Gather information.
- Address safety aspects.
- Address questions by school staff.
- Access community resources.
- Instill confidence in the family.
- Establish a monitoring process.

Community Resources

Lambton

STARRting Points, 336-0120

St. Clair Child and Youth Centre, 337-3701

Pathways Health Centre for Children, 542-3471

Community Care Access Centre, 337-1000

Local Association for Community Living

Kent

Prism Centre for Audiology & Children's Rehabilitation, 354-0520

Chatham-Kent Children's Services, 351-8454

Community Care Access Centre, 436-2222

Rain and Shine Behavioural Counselling Ltd., 255-1691

South West Regional Autism Program for Pre-schoolers, 358-1451

Local Association for Community Living

Lambton Kent District School Board
Autism Transition Committee

Lambton Kent
District School Board
Student Achievement ✓ Community Achievement Success

Transitional Supports for Students with Autism Spectrum Disorder

*"Coming together is a beginning.
Keeping together is progress.
Working together is success."*

Henry Ford

Lambton Kent District School Board
200 Wellington Steet
Sarnia, Ontario, N7T 7L2
Phone: (519) 336-1500   Fax: (519) 336-0992

(continued)

(continued)

What Is Autism?

Autism is a developmental disability that typically appears during the first three years of life.

The result of a neurological disorder that affects functioning of the brain, Autism Spectrum Disorder and its associated behaviours interferes with the normal development of the brain in the areas of reasoning, social interaction, and communication skills.

Children and adults with autism typically have deficiencies in verbal and non-verbal communications, social interactions, and leisure or play activities. The disorder makes it hard for them to communicate with others and relate to the outside world. They have a very difficult time accepting any sort of change in their daily routine, which may cause outbursts.

Inclusion

The board supports a philosophy of inclusion and a range of services and practices for special needs students. Regardless of placement option, students with special needs are an integral part of their school community and are supported by a team approach.

Practical Suggestions for Administrators

When a parent/guardian calls:

- Be welcoming.

- Explain the board's process for admitting special needs students.

- Ask if there has been an actual diagnosis and what, if any, medications are being taken.

- Research the student's educational history, including IEP.

- Determine what community services are being used.

- Discuss any behavioural concerns, the degree of intervention required and the support currently in place.

- Establish transportation requirements.

- Contact or visit the student's current educational setting.

- Discuss services and programs available in our system.

- For students who require significant support, arrange a school-based team meeting.

- Arrange a school visit with the parent, student, and support staff in the spring to familiarize the student with the new school environment.

Be prepared when a parent/guardian calls:

- Find out what other services are available (occupational therapy, behaviour support, physiotherapy, community support).

- Be familiar with board specialists who can provide assistance that will benefit both students and school staff.

- Find out about transportation for special needs students.

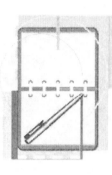

3. Survey for Parents

Triple A

Dear Parents:

Thank you very much for your cooperation and participation in Triple A. We hope that you have found the process helpful for your child's entry to school. In order for us to plan for next year, we would appreciate if you would complete the following:

1. Your hopes for this year are: _____

   _____

2. How do you feel about those hopes now?_____

   _____

3. Your worst fear for this year was: _____

   _____

4. How do you feel about those fears now?_____

   _____

   Do you have any other comments about your child's and his or her school's

   participation in Triple A? _____

   _____

   _____

5.

	Disagree				Agree
I feel Triple A has helped my child to have a smoother entry to school this year.	1	2	3	4	5
I believe Triple A is an effective program.	1	2	3	4	5
Triple A is difficult for school teams to implement.	1	2	3	4	5
My child's school team have learned new strategies through Triple A.	1	2	3	4	5

Halton Catholic District School Board

4. Student's Day at School

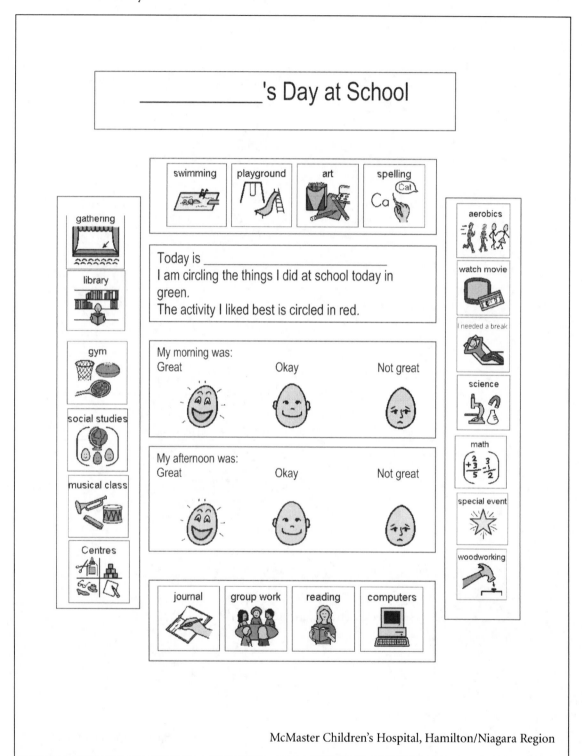

_____'s Day at School

swimming | playground | art | spelling

gathering

library

gym

social studies

musical class

Centres

Today is _____
I am circling the things I did at school today in green.
The activity I liked best is circled in red.

My morning was:
Great   Okay   Not great

My afternoon was:
Great   Okay   Not great

aerobics

watch movie

I needed a break

science

math

special event

woodworking

journal | group work | reading | computers

McMaster Children's Hospital, Hamilton/Niagara Region

5. School Communication

School Communication
To be completed daily by the classroom teacher and sent home

Activities	Yes	No	Comments

Homework that needs to be completed:

_____

_____

Additional comments:

_____

_____

McMaster Children's Hospital, Hamilton/Niagara Region

6. Information Pamphlet on ASD

Supporting Students

With

Autism Spectrum Disorder

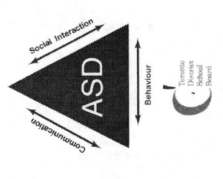

| Autism | PDD/NOS | Asperger Syndrome |

PDD/ASD Team
Toronto District School Board

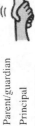

How Do I Teach a Student with Autism?

- Be positive.
- Get to know the child. Spending time intially will save you time in the long run.
- Be aware of individual differences, e.g., activity level, sensory needs, communication, and cognitive ability.
- Find strengths and needs of the student, e.g., make a list of likes and dislikes.
- Talk to parents/guardian, previous teachers, consultants.
- Read the O.S.R.
- Be specific with instruction.
- Limit your language.
- Be consistent, incorporating flexibility.
- Use direct language.
- Do not take responses personally.

Who Can Help You?

- Parent/guardian
- Principal
- MART/SERT
- Family of school consultant
- School support team
- PDD/ASD team
- SEAC (Special Education Advisory Committee)

Resources

Websites

Autism Society Ontario www.autismsociety.on.ca
Autism Intervention and Strategies for Success www.cesa7.k12.wi.us/sped/
Bridges www.bridges.canada.com – technology, training materials
Do to Learn http://dotolearn.com – free games, activities, and instruction on how to build a story strip
Geneva Centre www.autism.net – TDSB employees are members of the Geneva Centre
Internet Resources on Autism www.autism.org
Linda Hodgdon www.UseVisualStrategies.com
Mayer-Johnson LLC http://mayer-johnson.com
Parent Books www.parentbooks.ca
Queens University www.autismresearch.ca – current research
Carol Gray's Website www.thegraycentre.org
Tin Snips – activities and resources for teachers http://members.cox.net/tinsnips/welcome.html
Tippet Library (TDSB) http://media.tdsb.on.ca

Videotapes

Meet My Brother – Autism Society of Ontario
Straight Talk about Autism – Geneva Centre
Look Beyond the Labels – MTSB and Tippet Library

Books

Attwood, T. (1998) *Asperger's Syndrome: A Guide for Parents and Paraprofessionals.* London and Philadelphia: Jessica Kingsley Publishers
Hodgdon, L. (1995) *Visual Strategies for Improving Communication: Vol. 1 Practical Supports for Schools and Home.* Troy, MI: Quirk Roberts Publishing
Kluth, P. (2003) *You're Going to Love This Kid: Teaching Students with Autism in the Inclusive Classroom.* Baltimore. London and Sydney: Paul H. Brookes Publishing Co. Ltd.
Quill, K. (1995) *Teaching Children with Autism: Strategies to Enhance Communication and Socialization.* Albany, NY: Delmar Publishing Co.

(continued)

(continued)

AUTISM SPECTRUM DISORDER (ASD)

is a lifelong neurological condition that causes impairment in these three areas known as the triad of impairment

Students with autism present a myriad of strengths and abilities.

Communication Challenges

Receptive Language

- Comprehension
- Interpretation of verbal/non-verbal information
- Understanding abstract language
- Maintaining attention/changing focus rapidly

Expressive Language

- Limited vocabulary (students repeat prompted language)
- Echolalia (students with echolalia may present as functionally verbal)
- Improper use of pronouns, questions, statements
- Unusual tone or rhythm of speech
- Use of scripts, e.g., lines from movies repeated out of context

Pragmatics

Affects both Receptive and Expressive Language

- Interpreting non-verbal cues, e.g., body language, facial expression
- Maintaining a specific topic
- Relating comments in appropriate situations
- Turn taking in a conversation

Behaviour Issues

Restricted Repetitive Interests/Activities

- Preoccupation with specific interests, e.g., train schedules
- Excessive need for sameness, e.g., adherence to routines
- Lack of functional use of objects, e.g., lining up toys, spinning wheels
- Unusual body movements or repetitive behaviours, e.g., rocking, flicking fingers
- Limited coping strategies
- Inability to regulate arousal level
- Inflexible thinking

Contributors to Anxiety

- Dealing with unexpected events
- Accepting changes at home/school
- Adapting to new situations
- Understanding responses of others

Behaviours May Be Indicating

- A need for attention, "Look at me"
- An attempt to have tangible needs met, e.g., "I want ...", "I'm hungry", "I'm tired"
- A need to escape, "I don't understand this and I want to do something else"
- An attempt to regulate sensory stimulation, e.g., "It is too loud in here"

Social Interactions

- Knowing how to initiate an interaction
- Maintaining an interaction
- Recognizing the presence of others
- Understanding people's feelings and perspective
- Developing friendships
- Understanding unwritten social rules
- Demonstrating limited/unusual emotional responses
- Sustaining a conversation

Social Skills

Specific social skills should be taught in context in a variety of settings, e.g., recess, lunch and classroom setting.

ALL THREE AREAS OF IMPAIRMENT INTERCONNECT AND ARE NOT MUTUALLY EXCLUSIVE

7. Critical Information Sheet

School Support Program
Autism Spectrum Disorders

Critical Information Sheet at a Glance

Student Name: _____ **Teacher:** _____ **Grade:** _____

Communication	Reinforcers	Sensitivities	Descriptions of Challenging (Target) Behaviour
How does student communicate? Verbally: Yes No PECS: Yes No Sign language: Yes No Combination of above: Yes No None of above: Yes No How does student let you know: • Wants/Needs _____ • Protest/Refusal _____ • Assistance _____ • To stop _____ • Need for bathroom _____ • Sick _____ Is a visual schedule used? Yes No How do you provide information? Visual references: ____ Pictures: ____ Objects: ____ Signs: ____ Gestures: ____ Strengths of student (list three): _____ _____ _____	List highly preferred/interesting likes/reinforcers. Items: _____ _____ Verbal: _____ Social: _____ _____ Foods: _____ _____ Sounds/Music: _____ Activities: _____ _____ Does student take medication, have allergies, have a special diet? _____ _____	Is change a challenge for student? Yes/No Can student become overwhelmed by noise? Yes/No _____ Does student express emotions? Yes/No If yes, list and describe how: _____ _____ Does student need assistance with bathroom, eating, other? Yes/No If yes, please specify: _____ _____ Does student follow a modified program (academic modification) or are accommodations made to learning (use of computer, class positioning, etc.)? Yes/No If yes, please list: _____ _____	Are specific behaviours observed that would define student's target behaviour? (Describe in detail, as if to a stranger.) _____ _____ _____ What do you do/say/not say to help settle student (re-direct, relaxation, key phrases, etc.)? _____ _____ How do you know behaviour has increased? _____ _____ If student is physically aggressive, what do you do/say/not say? _____ _____ Is there need for a safety plan? Yes No

Thames Valley Children's Centre

Thames Valley Children's Centre, South West Region

8. Student Profile

Student Profile

The Student		
	What **things** does the student like?	What **things** does the student dislike?
	What **activities** does the student enjoy?	What **activities** does the student NOT enjoy?
	In which activity, game, or sport does the student do well?	In which activity, game, or sport does the student need help?

Strengths	Interests	Needs

(continued)

(continued)

2

Student Profile

This is a list of events or situations the student may find stressful, and some strategies that may help.

Stressors	Strategies

Documentation:

This student has a safety plan: yes _____ no _____ that is _____ /
is not _____ included.

Specify incidents that need to be documented:

_____

_____

_____

9. Promoting Independence

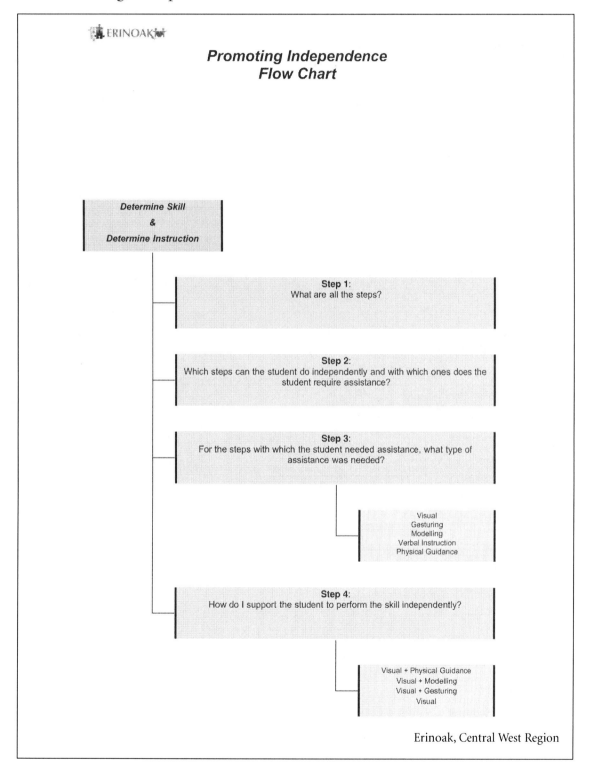

10. Inventory of Functional Skills

Sample Form   **INVENTORY/ASSESSMENT OF FUNCTIONAL SKILLS**
IN SECONDARY SCHOOLS

Student: _____   School: _____

Teacher: _____   Support staff: _____

Inventory completed by: _____   Date: _____

Rubric/Evaluation Criteria

S	= Spontaneous	• Task/skill is self-initiated and completed independently.
C	= Cue	• Task/skill is completed independently with cues (e.g., pictorial/visual supports, pointing). Identify the type of cue – be specific.
PG	= Partial Guide	• Task/skill is completed with partial physical guides/partial prompts (e.g., some hand-over-hand modelling, physical gestures). Identify the type of partial guide – be specific.
FG	= Full Guide	• Task/skill is completed with full physical guides/prompts (e.g., full hand-over-hand).
	N.A.	• Task/skill is not applicable OR other person completes the task/skill.

1. SCHOOL ARRIVAL

a) Entry Routine

	S	C	PG	FG	NA	COMMENTS
Get off bus with backpack						
Walk toward school						
Open school door						
Enter school building						
Greet familiar adults or peers						
Go to office/guidance office for admit or late slips (if necessary)						

b) Locker Routine

	S	C	PG	FG	NA	COMMENTS
Walk to locker area OR wait to meet friend(s) and walk together						
Find own locker						
Remove mitts/gloves and place in pocket of jacket						
Open lock and pull lock open						
Remove lock						
Open locker door						
Place lock on hook						

2

c) **Organization and Life Skills**

	S	C	PG	FG	NA	COMMENTS
Remove backpack and place on floor						
Open backpack, remove lunch and put in locker						
Remove hat/jacket (e.g., unzip/unbutton)						
Hang hat/jacket on hook in locker						
Take off boots and place on locker floor						
Get shoes from locker/backpack						
Put on shoes						

	S	C	PG	FG	NA	COMMENTS
Review timetable on inside of locker door						
Gather books for morning classes and place in backpack						
Pick up lock						
Close locker door						
Insert lock						
Snap lock shut						

	S	C	PG	FG	NA	COMMENTS
Check watch for time to go to class						
Hang out at locker with friends till warning bell OR go to homeroom						
Interact with friends						
Drink from water fountain in hallway – wait till fountain is free						

2. **LIFE SKILLS – PERSONAL CARE**

a) **Washroom Routines**

	S	C	PG	FG	NA	COMMENTS
Go to designated washroom (male/female) with backpack						
Open washroom door and enter						
Find empty cubicle and enter OR wait till cubicle is free						
Close and lock cubicle door						
Place backpack on floor or hang on hook						
Complete toileting – use toilet paper, flush, etc.						
Get backpack						
Unlock cubicle door and exit						
Use tissue and place in trash when finished						
Wash and dry hands at sink – use paper towels and place in trash can OR use mechanical hand dryer						

Secondary School Inventory

(continued)

(continued)

3

b) Grooming

	S	C	PG	FG	NA	COMMENTS
Enter washroom						
Get comb/brush from backpack						
Look in mirror and comb/brush hair						
Put comb/brush in backpack						
Adjust clothing						
Exit washroom						

3. ROTATION

a) Hallways

	S	C	PG	FG	NA	COMMENTS
Carry backpack (e.g., by hand, over shoulders)						
Walk to class						
Walk on right side of hallway						
Adjust walking pace depending on traffic (e.g., slow down, walk faster)						
Walk with traffic						
Walk around crowds or wait till crowd disperses						
Climb up or down staircase (on right side)						

b) Doorways

	S	C	PG	FG	NA	COMMENTS
Open doors (as needed) OR hold onto open door if opened by others						
Walk through doorway						
Hold onto open door if others are walking through						

4. CLASSROOM ROUTINES

a) Entry Routine

	S	C	PG	FG	NA	COMMENTS
Find classroom door						
Open classroom door						
Enter classroom						
Hand teacher note/homework (as appropriate)						
Give teacher message (if applicable)						
Find own desk and sit in chair						
Place backpack on back of chair or floor						
Participate in Opening Exercises in homeroom or first class (e.g., stand for anthem, respond when name called for attendance, listen to announcements)						
Interact with classmates (as appropriate)						

Secondary School Inventory

4

5. <u>LEARNING STRATEGIES</u>

a) <u>Organization Skills</u>

	S	C	PG	FG	NA
Open backpack					
Remove materials for class (textbook, binder, pencil case, etc.)					
Open binder to appropriate subject					
Remain sitting in chair at desk					
Interact with friends till class begins (as appropriate)					

<u>COMMENTS</u>

b) <u>Homework</u>

	S	C	PG	FG	NA
Remain sitting in chair at desk					
Open binder to appropriate subject					
Find previous day's homework					
Participate in taking up homework (e.g., follow oral questions/answers, check own written answers, make corrections as needed)					
Answer question(s) when called upon					
Raise hand to offer answer(s), wait until called upon					
Lower hand if not called upon for answer(s)					
Advocate on behalf of self (e.g., request assistance, clarification)					

<u>COMMENTS</u>

c) <u>Lesson</u>

	S	C	PG	FG	NA
Attend to lesson and presentation of materials					
Remain on task during oral lesson					
Answer question(s) when called upon					
Raise hand to offer answer(s), wait until called upon					
Lower hand if not called upon for answer(s)					
Advocate on behalf of self (e.g., request assistance, clarification)					

<u>COMMENTS</u>

d) <u>Seatwork</u>

	S	C	PG	FG	NA
Pass out worksheet (e.g., pass back, pass forward)					
Take worksheet(s) papers when passed out					
Show politeness and courtesy (please, thank-you)					

<u>COMMENTS</u>

Secondary School Inventory

(continued)

(continued)

5

d) Seatwork (cont'd)

	S	C	PG	FG	NA
Remove item(s) from pencil case as needed (e.g., pencil/pen, eraser, ruler, correction fluid, pencil sharpener)					
Sharpen pencil (e.g., portable or class sharpener)					
Write name and date on worksheet					
Advocate on behalf of self (e.g., request assistance, clarification)					
Open binder to take out blank sheet and close binder					
Copy from board					
Complete assigned task(s)					
Move from one seatwork activity/task to another					
Use eraser and correction fluid as appropriate					
Raise hand to request help if needed					
Put completed seatwork in designated area					
Put marked/unmarked work in appropriate place(s)					
Copy homework into agenda book					

COMMENTS

e) Group Work

	S	C	PG	FG	NA
Move chair and desk to form small group					
Participate in group discussion (small and large groups)					
Participate in presentation of project					

COMMENTS

f) Organization and Class Dismissal

	S	C	PG	FG	NA
Clear desk (e.g., put materials away in backpack)					
Refer to timetable to check about next class					
Line up at door					
Interact with classmates					
Leave classroom when bell rings or when dismissed by teacher					
Go to next class					

COMMENTS

Secondary School Inventory

11. Autism Transitional Classroom

The Autism Transitional Classroom

The Autism Transitional Classroom creates the opportunity for treatment providers and educators to bridge the gap between treatment and special education, and to give students who have an Autism Spectrum Disorder the intensive support required to function successfully in an educational setting. Specifically, the transitional aspects of the treatment program focus on teaching educators basic intervention skills and a method for translating them into special education strategies. This demands a very strong commitment of staff time from the school board, based on the idea that the amount of time committed by the school board will match the size of the child's need. The partnership between Chatham-Kent Children's Services and the St. Clair Catholic District School Board, with the support of the Ministry of Education, provides an opportunity for professionals, children, and families to meet these challenges.

The formal criteria for admission to the classroom require that the child has a diagnosis of an autistic disorder or other pervasive developmental disorder made by a qualified registered psychologist. In addition, the child must be referred to the program by the CKCS Autism Team or the St. Clair Catholic District School Board, and be a client of the CKCS Autism Team. The program, housed onsite at Chatham-Kent Children's Services, consists of one classroom and one teacher with space for six full-time equivalent students. The CKCS Autism Team provides clinical support to the program. Consideration is given to students whose current school placement breaks down in such a way that training or retraining of that student and his/her resource team has a high probability of restoring the success of the child's current placement.

The Autism Transitional Classroom's primary goal is to provide a program that is:
   1) designed to translate treatment goals and techniques into special education strategies that, through intensive training, can be implemented by school personnel within the context of an IEP;
   2) individualized; and
   3) based on the scientific principles of applied behaviour analysis (ABA) and reinforcement.
As the name implies, the program aims to help educators teach children with Autism Spectrum Disorders by providing temporary but very intensive supports to the educational professionals to adapt and apply the special education strategies in the least intrusive environment possible. Hence, the intervention is client-centred, seeks to create innovative learning environments within schools across Chatham-Kent, and celebrates the achievements of students and professionals alike.

Description of the Autism Transitional Classroom Training Program
All treatment and training provided by the CKCS Autism Team is based on the scientific principles and data supporting the approach known as *applied behaviour analysis (ABA).* The best practice application of this clinical philosophy is known as *intensive behavioural intervention (IBI).* Funded regional autism service programs provide treatment based on ABA/IBI, and in keeping with the idea of an unbroken continuum of service, the Autism Transitional Classroom program is based on these same principles.

(continued)

(continued)

The program is intensive and uses individually administered techniques to meet the needs of children with higher needs, often those with a dual diagnosis of autism and a developmental disability. The Essential Transitional Curriculum (ETC) provides special education programming using behavioural intervention techniques that are translated into individualized special education strategies. The educational staff are taught how to individualize programs for each child, how to make the materials to implement the programs, and how to maintain the programs so that they grow with the child.

Professional Development and Guidance of the Educational Program
The staff training model embedded in the Essential Transitional Curriculum means that the primary day-to-day resource for the teacher, educational assistant, and resource staff in the program is the CKCS clinical staff. Therefore, professional development for educators occurs constantly and is one of the primary goals of the Autism Transitional Classroom. The program requires consultation and guidance from an educator with extensive knowledge of the procedures, regulations, and practices surrounding the IEP process.

Multidisciplinary Planning of the Child's Program
The Autism Transitional Classroom draws on the full resources of the CKCS Autism Team, which includes a psychologist, senior therapist, two child and family consultants, two lead therapists, four instructor/therapists, and an autism support worker. The St. Clair Catholic District School Board provides a classroom teacher, educational assistant, and team support.

a) The target skill must be essential to the child's adjustment to a *classroom environment*, whether that is a special education classroom with a relatively small number of students or a regular classroom with a larger number of students.
b) The teaching program and materials must resemble special education teaching strategies and materials more closely than they resemble specialized treatment strategies and materials.
c) The programs must be written so that a "typical" educational assistant or other special education resource staff member with no prior knowledge of treatment principles or techniques can learn to implement them.
d) The programs must meet the child's learning needs in ways that are either compatible with or do not disrupt the teaching of other children in the classroom, unless an isolated teaching environment is both required *and* available.
e) The programs must match the parameters/requirements of the formal IEP process.

Planning and Coordination of Transition from the Autism Transitional Classroom to Local Schools
As the name "Autism Transitional Classroom" implies, the entire focus of this project is to create a process for helping children to make this transition. The model is designed to allow educators to practise and master the skills needed to assemble and implement the resources required by children with Autism Spectrum Disorders. Transition planning involves the receiving school staff visiting the classroom for training, the Autism Transitional Classroom attending at the home school to provide support, and parent involvement in the entire process.

12. Think Tank on Autism

Toronto
District
School
Board

The TDSB's Think Tank on Autism (May 2006)
Report of Findings

Executive Summary

Prepared for The Toronto District School Board, August 2006
by Denyse Gregory, Research & Evaluation Consultant

In May 2006, the Toronto District School Board (TDSB) conducted a Think Tank on Autism to address issues related to the education of students with Autism Spectrum Disorders (ASD) in the TDSB. The purpose of the Think Tank was to bring together a cross-section of people from various stakeholder groups to gain from their collective wisdom.

The session featured representation from parents and students, parent and student advocates, the medical profession, government, universities, agencies, the Ontario Human Rights Commission, and a variety of staff from the TDSB and other neighbouring boards.

The agenda was designed to raise awareness, establish collaborative networks, share best practices, improve accessibility, collaboratively problem-solve, and create positive momentum to move forward to support student success.

The report of the findings of the event summarized the discussions that took place that day, as well as the feedback of the participants about the Think Tank process itself. The greatest challenge in the reporting was that the diversity of the stakeholders participating in the Think Tank naturally resulted in a wide variety of perspectives and insights. Nevertheless, a number of themes emerged repeatedly in the feedback provided. The key themes are summarized below.

Defining Success for Students on the Autism Spectrum

Participants defined "success" for students on the autism spectrum in a variety of ways. The most prevalent were improvements in the following student outcomes:
- improved social skills and relationships with peers;
- enhanced emotional well-being (e.g., self-confidence, attitude toward school and comfort level);
- increased academic progress;
- life skills learnings (e.g., independence and communication skills); and
- improved transitions to regular schooling or to post-secondary options.

Factors Contributing to Student Success

➤ **Students' Strengths:**
Participants identified a multitude of the strengths of students with ASD that contributed to their success. The most prevalent of these were:
- personal characteristics such as motivation, perseverance, and a strong sense of self; and
- learning strengths such as effective communication skills (in particular, strong verbal skills),
- strong academic skills, and an ability to work cooperatively with their peers.

➤ **Programs and Services:**
Participants identified a variety of programs and services that they believed contributed to the success of students on the autism spectrum. The most prevalent of these were:
- holistic, child-centred programming, characterized by features such as the identification of students' individual needs and strengths, utilization of a variety of strategies and approaches, and the involvement of TDSB support services;

(continued)

(continued)

- a supportive home environment in which the student's parents are actively involved and engaged as partners with the school;
- a supportive school environment that involves the direct support and involvement of teachers, EAs, resource teachers, and support services (e.g., psychologists and speech language pathologists); and
- partnerships with community agencies such as Surrey Place Centre and The Geneva Centre for Autism.

Recommendations

Participants offered a variety of valuable suggestions and recommendations for next steps, both immediate and long-term. The most predominant of these were as follows:

➤ Expand professional development and training opportunities for teachers, EAs, support staff, and administrators to increase awareness and understanding and to improve service delivery for all of those working with students on the autism spectrum.

➤ Continue the dialogue with other professionals and parents to understand autism better and to identify ways to improve program delivery and support for students with ASD.

➤ Employ a more coordinated, team approach to enhance program delivery in all schools by:
- increasing the focus on the identification of each child's particular needs;
- enhancing the in-house support available to students with ASD (e.g., EAs, occupational therapists, language pathologists, and ABA training);
- establishing PDD/ASD teams in all four quadrants and assigning a "case manager" to coordinate program delivery within each family of schools or quadrant;
- fostering partnerships and communication with parents; and
- fostering partnerships/collaboration with community service providers or agencies to maximize awareness and use of the available resources.

➤ Provide greater support for families of students on the autism spectrum to empower them in the process of educating their child. This includes informing parents about the options available to them, providing or connecting them to outreach programs to support families, and facilitating crisis management for families.

➤ Promote acceptance and tolerance of diversity within the education system and within the community as a whole. Specifically, it was suggested that the TDSB and community partners take steps to "combat the stigma of ASD" and to "debunk the myths" of ASD.

The Think Tank Process

Participants in the Think Tank on Autism were given an opportunity to comment on the Think Tank process via an online feedback form. In general, respondents rated the Think Tank on Autism session as **very engaging**. The content was rated as **helpful** and **very relevant**. Finally, the format of the day was thought to be **conducive to dialogue and to the sharing of ideas**.

Respondents' comments suggested that they appreciated the opportunity to work together with the various stakeholder groups. As articulated by one of the respondents, "The session was a good example of how it is possible for different stakeholders to work together for the common good of students with exceptionalities."

13. Resources for Drivers

 Brant Haldimand Norfolk Catholic District School Board

Ensuring a Successful Transition:
A Resource for Transportation Drivers

The Brant Haldimand Norfolk Catholic District School Board recognizes the many challenges students with Autism Spectrum Disorder (ASD) face with the transition from home to school and school to home. We appreciate the fact that the bus drive to and from school can have a direct impact on how successful the day will be. Thus, in conjunction with the ASD School Support Program, a resource is being developed to assist transportation drivers with this very important transition.

After consultation with the transportation department, drivers were asked to identify their needs when transporting students with ASD. Areas of greatest concern included strategies to assist with difficult behaviours, prevention of bullying, communication techniques between home/school/bus, and a heightened understanding of the disorder.

The transportation resource initiative will include a teaching component and the creation of a resource based on drivers' needs. The teaching component will include in-service training that will provide an overview of ASD, specifically focusing on the characteristics that might lead to difficulties on the bus. Scenarios describing frequently observed behaviours on the bus and specific strategies to assist the student with ASD will also be presented. Strategies to be discussed include:

- Prearranged visits with the school
- Social narratives and schedules
- Recognizing anxious behaviour and how to deal with it
- The use of visuals
- Reinforcement systems
- Buddy system
- Identifying the behavioural triggers of a student with ASD
- Home/school/bus–school/home communication sheet
- Consistent seating
- Rules on the bus
- Sameness and predictability
- Tangible activities that can occupy students on the bus
- Creation of an emergency plan

Three possible resources are currently being created for transportation drivers. The resources, which will be introduced at an in-service, are as follows:

1. A chart-style resource, which can be laminated and posted on the bus, that includes essential information such as:
   - an overview of ASD;
   - a list of behaviours that may occur on the bus; and
   - a list of strategies to assist the ASD student with these behaviours.

2. A smaller version of the chart that can be laminated and placed on the visor above the driver's seat. Information will include a list of behaviours with accompanying strategies. The driver simply flips down the visor and has quick reference to strategies.

3. Small laminated cards that can be placed on a key ring so that transportation drivers can wear it on their belt loop as a quick reference guide to behavioural strategies.

A simple communication sheet has also been developed to facilitate communication between parents, transportation drivers, and school staff. This resource would provide essential information to ensure successful transitions from setting to setting.

14. Transportation Visuals

Brant Haldimand Norfolk Catholic District School Board

15. Autism Demonstration Site

Avon Maitland District School Board
Autism Demonstration Site

In 2003–2004 the Avon Maitland District School Board established an "Autism Demonstration Site". The goal of this site is to provide classroom teachers, educational assistants, principals, and vice-principals access to personnel with hands-on experience dealing with students who have been diagnosed within the Autism Spectrum.

❖ Visitors to the site interact with specially trained Autism Demonstration Site staff via a tour of individual classrooms and a small-group presentation format.

❖ The purpose of the tour is to model the creation of appropriate environments, implementation of specialized teaching strategies, and successful, research-based behaviour management techniques. This is achieved through direct observation of students and teachers in action. The observation includes students in regular primary classroom settings as well as specialized classroom settings.

❖ The small-group presentation primarily includes an overview of the essential aspects of a student's profile within the autism spectrum and related educational implications, a description of available district resource materials, and a Q&A session.

❖ On each tour date, the site is supported by the school's assigned speech and language pathologist, the special education consultant, and an ASD consultant from the Thames Valley Children's Centre.

❖ Since its inception, approximately 40 people a year have taken advantage of the opportunity to visit the site.

❖ Participants have commented on the extensive knowledge base of the Autism Demonstration Site staff, the opportunity to see appropriate materials and resources, the benefits of first-hand viewing of specialized teaching strategies, and practical sensory room ideas on a budget!

16. Strategies Checklist

STUDENT:_____   DATE:_____

Strategies List

Environmental	Communication	Instructional
○ intensive support ○ study carrel/alternative space ○ small-group support ○ limit adults involved ○ modified schedule/day ○ consistent daily routine ○ minimize transitions ○ keep familiar, acquired activities in the program as new ones are added ○ visual organizers ○ priming ○ prepare for changes ○ alter physical arrangement of room ○ provide adaptive equipment ○ strategic seating ○ preferential coat hook/locker position ○ chair/mat/seating ○ visual timer ○ reduce distraction and sensory overloads ○ sensory breaks ○ supervision during unstructured events	○ use concrete and specific language ○ clarify idioms, words with double meanings ○ slow down language – one command at a time, short, clear phrases ○ break tasks into smaller steps ○ use gestures, modelling, and demonstrations with verbalizations ○ write down requests, instructions ○ engage attention visually, verbally, and physically before giving information ○ watch and listen to response attempt – respond positively to any attempt ○ model correct format ○ provide alternative forms of communication ○ use visual cues to support understanding ○ provide scripts for language	○ use the student's strengths ○ apply learning to real situations ○ rote learning ○ visual supports ○ maintain context, vary content ○ present new concepts in a concrete manner ○ divide instruction into small, sequential steps ○ reduce/chunk information ○ written instructions ○ highlight key information ○ colour code materials ○ indicate start and stop of activity ○ preteach vocabulary, skills ○ duplicated notes ○ computer assisted learning ○ timer/time management aids ○ graphic organizers ○ structured cooperative experiences ○ instructor proximity
Motivational	Self-Regulation	Assessment
○ visual cues ○ meaningful experiences ○ ensure comprehension ○ utilize student's interests ○ immediate feedback ○ first ... then strategy ○ naturally occurring reinforcers ○ vary reinforcers and provide choice of reinforcers ○ reinforce any attempt towards goals and objectives ○ encourage, accept, and teach choice making ○ invite and encourage natural initiation of tasks ○ visual timer	○ direct instruction ○ safe person ○ communication book ○ tracking sheet ○ teach relaxation strategies ○ redirection ○ distraction ○ tangible rewards ○ praise ○ immediate feedback ○ first ... then strategy ○ red ... green strategy ○ social narratives ○ comic strip conversations ○ an item a day	○ apply learning to real situations ○ shorten or alter activities ○ provide choice of activity for assessment ○ teach format ahead of time through rehearsal ○ wait time for processing or task completion ○ allow oral responses ○ scribe answers for student ○ provide visual cues as a way to teach how to summarize or write ○ break the assessment into smaller chunks and spread out testing ○ editing support ○ calculator/matrix ○ alternative setting ○ incidental assessment

Waterloo Region District School Board

17. Classroom Layout

**Creating an Autism-Friendly Classroom:
The Classroom Layout**

The classroom itself can be set up to support the student's learning and minimize challenging behaviours. A visually organized classroom can support the learner in orienting himself or herself and can help the learner navigate the learning environment.

Furniture Placement:

- ❏ Lay out furniture to create boundaries that support learning, minimize distractions, and facilitate transitions.
- ❏ Use furniture, carpets, tape, shelving units, filing cabinets, etc., to make activity areas clearly visible and regulate traffic flow.
- ❏ Minimize wide open areas to reduce running in physically active students who have difficulty with transitions.
- ❏ Locate free choice and leisure time areas away from exits.
- ❏ Be consistent about the location of workstations and learning centres.
- ❏ Clearly mark different areas with meaningful visual cues.
- ❏ Initially use learning centres only for their designated purposes to teach relevance and provide predictable structure.
- ❏ Plan for multiple activities occurring simultaneously with the least distraction.
- ❏ Provide a quiet place for students to get away from distractions and stimulation and take a break if they need to.

Traffic Patterns:

- ❏ Mark traffic flow of students and staff clearly to meet the learner's needs by reducing wait times.
- ❏ Mark arrows or footprints on the floor to show students how to get from one area to another.
- ❏ Try to match the flow of traffic in the room to the daily routines.

Storage:

- ❏ Make instructional and reward items easily and immediately accessible without being inadvertently distracting.
- ❏ Consider labelling work/activity bins on the outside with pictures, the item, or symbols that the student will understand.

Surrey Place Centre, Toronto Region

(continued)

(continued)

Visual Supports:

❑ Present visuals at the students' eye level.
❑ Make visuals available in locations that will support appropriate behaviour. Consider both posting visuals outside the classroom and carrying them.
❑ Make sure that images selected are specific to the event or activity you want to depict. Students with ASD can be easily distracted by unrelated details, so be careful about what is "accidentally" in your picture.
❑ Make sure that rules are posted in problem areas. If there is not a specific location, either post rules at eye level in central locations of the class or carry them.
❑ Limit clutter in the classroom. Limit materials in areas where the student with ASD is required to concentrate (e.g., behind the teacher at circle time) so that the student can focus on your instructions and not on background distractions.
❑ Limit materials on bulletin boards. Try to remove materials as themes finish so that the current themes are most prominent, rather than keeping them on display for the school year.

Surrey Place Centre

18. Morning Routine

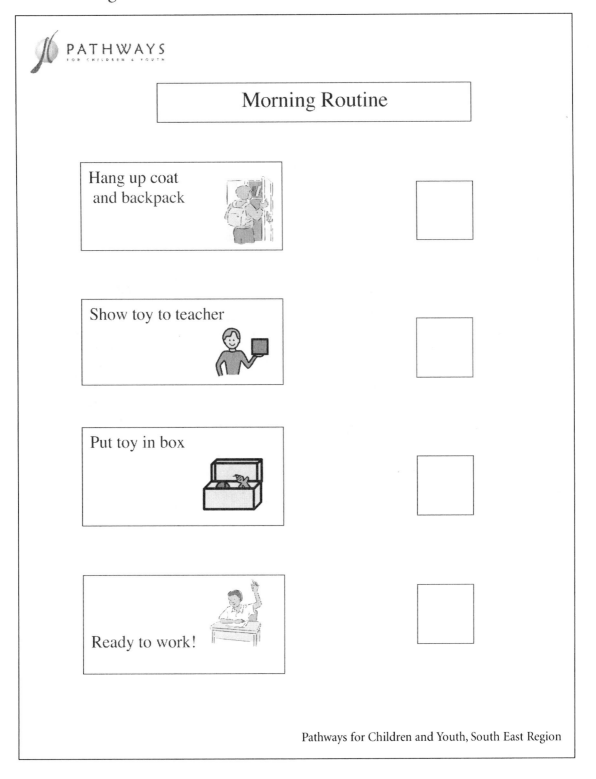

19. Safety Plan: Crisis Protocol

•peel District School Board

ASD Resource Team

Safety Plan: Crisis Protocol
Ensuring Positive School Environments

Name: _____   Date Developed: _____
Parent Contact: _____   Review Dates: _____
Emergency Contact: _____   _____

Unsafe Behaviour(s)	▪

Staff Expectation: Reduce talking, planned proximity (tone/volume/control)

Stage 1: Escalation	Escalating Behavioural Signals (Observable signs of increased anxiety/agitation)	
	Behaviour	Strategy
	1.	
	2.	
	3.	
	4.	

Stage 2: Crisis	Crisis Response	
	Adults to be called:	
	If	Then
	1.	
	2.	
	3.	
	4.	

Stage 3: Coping	Supported Self-Control (soothe and redirect)
	1.
	2.
	3.

Staff Training   First Aid: _____
                        Other: _____

Parent Signature: _____   Date: _____
Principal Signature: _____   Date: _____
Psychologist Signature: _____   Date: _____

20. Information for Occasional Teachers

CONFIDENTIAL

Student Information for Occasional Teachers

One of my students, _____, has a neurological condition known as **Autistic Spectrum Disorders** (ASD). As a result, certain things in the school setting are difficult for this student. Students with ASD typically have trouble in social situations and when their routine is changed.

The following is a list of situations that might be difficult for this student to handle:

The following is a list of behaviours the student might exhibit when feeling overwhelmed or under stress:

The following is a list of strategies you can use when you see the student exhibiting these behaviours:

Anxiety can be a serious problem for children with ASD, and it can escalate rapidly. If you notice this student doing any of the following:

_____

immediately ask _____ in room number _____ to help you.

Please do not try to handle this type of behaviour on your own because there are specific methods for doing so.

Waterloo Region District School Board

21. Suggestions to Support Transitions

Suggestions to Support Transitions

The following are suggestions that may offer additional support to students who have a difficult time with transitions. The goal of these suggestions is to make the transition process a positive experience for all involved.

Suggestions:

- Have the student meet all of the teachers that will be teaching the student in the upcoming year.

- Take pictures of each of the teachers to put into a mini photo album. Label the pictures with the teachers' names and the subjects they teach.

- Create checklists for each subject (e.g., what tools are needed to be successful in class).

- Create a map of the school that includes routes to each class.

- Assign a locker to the student.

- Have a support person in place to greet the student upon arrival at the classroom. Have the support person accompany the student en route to the next class.

- Have the student follow a few days of the school cycle. Ideally, over a few days the student would have the opportunity to attend each class at least one time.

Kinark Child and Family Services, Central East Region

22. Preparing Students for a Special Event

Children's Hospital of Eastern Ontario
Centre hospitalier pour enfants de l'est de l'Ontario

10 Things to Remember When Preparing Students for a Special Event

1. Explain to your students what to expect from the event IN ADVANCE.

2. Set out guidelines and expectations of behaviour.

3. Give your student a predetermined "way out" if the student cannot cope.

4. Expose the student to the sights, sounds, and smells before the event – it can be overwhelming!

5. Ensure that you have an "emergency card" containing necessary information, including how to get help if needed.

6. Practise social interactions with social scripts so that the student can participate more easily.

7. Promote the maintenance of structured days throughout the holiday period (e.g., homework, schedules).

8. Use a calendar to show the student when he or she will be on holiday and when he or she will return to school.

9. Make a story of the actual event, holiday destination, or trip using pictures, photographs, etc.

10. Practise reading signs in the environment, particularly the signs for the toilets!

23. Task Sequence for Home Time

VISUAL SUPPORTS (Task Sequence)

		Home Time
1		I put my headset into my brown bag.
2		I line up.
3		I walk quietly into the hallway with my teacher.
4		I put my headset into my backpack.
5		I put on my coat.
6		I put on my boots.
7		I put on my hat and scarf.
8		I put on my gloves.
9		I put on my backpack.
10		I line up and wait for the bell to ring.
11		I walk with my teacher to the front door.
12		I wait for my mom to pick me up.
13		I walk to the car and say, "Hi, Mom".

Have the student check off each box on completion of each sequence.

Durham District School Board

24. Visuals for Transition from School to Home

Transition Tasks – School to Home

home time	get ready	tidy up
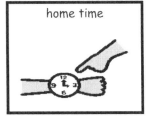		

open locker	get dressed	backpack
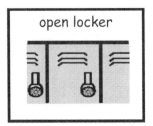		

close locker	line up	leave school

leave school	good-bye	school bus

Toronto Catholic District School Board

25. Visual Steps for Using Workout Room

Workout Room

1. Go to the workout room. __

2. Roll on the exercise ball. __

3. Squeeze bag and lift weights. __

4. Walk on the treadmill. __

5. Ride the bicycle. __

Toronto Catholic District School Board

26. Visuals for School Activities

School Activities

walk in hall 	walk 	classroom 
work 	workout room 	gym 
school library 	computer 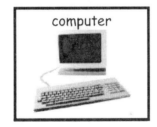	computer work 
field 	tidy up 	calendar 

Toronto Catholic District School Board

27. Visuals for Going to Work

Going to Work

make lunch	lunch in backpack	dress for outside
let's go to work	TTC bus	check in with boss
jobs	break	eat lunch
more jobs	see boss	pay
buy snack	TTC bus	school

Toronto Catholic District School Board

28. Bus Rules

BUS

1. Sit in your seat when the bus is moving.

2. Keep your hands inside the bus.

3. Walk in the aisle.

4. Use a quiet voice on the bus.

5. Keep your hands and feet to yourself.

Erinoak, Central West Region

29. Getting Ready for the Bus

Getting Ready for the Bus

Monday	Tuesday	Wednesday	Thursday	Friday

Tidy up my desk

Put my lunchbox away

Put my agenda away

Get my backpack

Put on my hat, coat, and mitts

Line up at the door

Algonquin Child and Family Services, North East Region

30. Individualized Daily Schedule

At a Glance
Individualized Daily Schedule

Students with ASD may have events that occur in their daily school life that might not be part of the typical schedules of many of their peers, yet these events are very important for the involved students. Such events might include a special transportation arrival time, medication times, or times devoted to work with educators other than the classroom teacher. This individualized daily schedule of what will happen most school days includes times, events, and locations, as well as any notes.

Schedule

Time	Event	Location	Important Information

McMaster
Children's Hospital

31. Monday Schedule

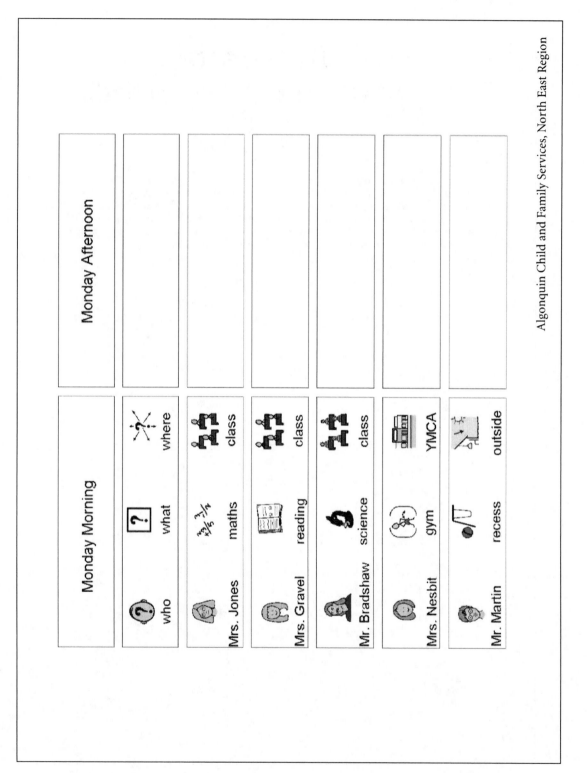

Algonquin Child and Family Services, North East Region

32. Classroom/Environment

CLASSROOM/ENVIRONMENT

Research has shown that there are links between the behaviour of a student with PDD and the environment within which the behaviour is exhibited. Inappropriate behaviour can be reduced or eliminated by making changes and/or adjustments to the environment. When setting up your classroom, do not forget that each student with PDD is different, and take into consideration their strengths and needs before making changes.

Classroom/environment adaptations:

- Be aware of any sensory stimuli within the areas and the possible effects on the student.
- Designate areas for individual/group learning.
- Designate a "break area" for the student to go to when he/she feels anxiety building up.
- Create clear boundaries (e.g., use bookshelves, filing cabinets, carpets, tape on the floor).
- Arrange the desks in the classroom so the student can easily navigate:
  - Make a clear path to the door, teacher, and all needed items that the student can access.
  - Have the student sit in front of or facing the teacher and schedules, but away from high-traffic areas, windows, and doors to reduce distractions.
  - Avoid having the student sit in the middle of a group that may cause conflicts and/or feelings of personal space invasion.
  - Place desks in groups to encourage social interactions.
- Provide a clear and predictable schedule.
- Use a colour-coding system (e.g., math is green).
- Provide choices for the student.
- Alternate more difficult and demanding tasks with easier and more enjoyable ones, and adapt tasks and materials to prevent student frustration.

School-wide considerations:

- Think about the classroom location in relation to potential distractions or sensory stimulations (e.g., cafeteria, gymnasium, washrooms).
- Prepare the student in advance for changes in routines (e.g., assembly, fire alarms, concerts).
- Define all other locations by clearly labelling them (e.g., library, gymnasium).
- Allow some flexibility in the schedule to reduce the student's anxiety (e.g., walk through the hallway between classes before the other students, go early to the locker room to get ready to go home).
- Take into consideration the safety of the student in the hallways and outside on the playground.

Child Care Resources, Northern Region

33. Ten Ways to Create Classroom Structure

CHEO Children's Hospital of Eastern Ontario
Centre hospitalier pour enfants de l'est de l'Ontario

10 Ways to Create Structure in Your Classroom

Students with ASD often function best in classrooms that offer a great deal of structure, both in terms of the physical layout of the room and expectations of the teacher or the assignment.

1. Use furniture, area rugs, or even electrical tape on the floor to separate the room into distinct areas.

2. Each area should have its own function (e.g., computer area, individual work area, play area).

3. Use signs to clearly indicate the function of each area.

4. Clearly label any ambiguous areas, materials, etc.

5. Label where all the student's belongings should be stored or where shared materials can be found.

6. Post a schedule of the day to give students advanced knowledge of what the day will bring.

7. Use this schedule to demonstrate any changes to the routine throughout the day.

8. Create a homework checklist to be filled out every day, complete with materials needed.

9. Colour code binders, notebooks, and required materials for each subject.

10. Use visual aids to support verbal instruction.

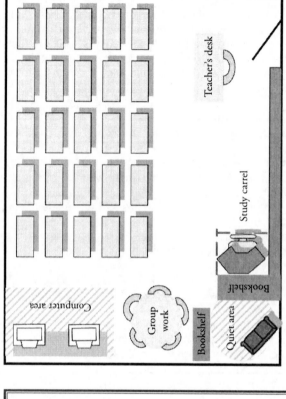

Computer area
Group work
Bookshelf
Quiet area
Bookshelf
Study carrel
Teacher's desk

Here you can see an example of a structured classroom. The layout of the room has been physically defined using area rugs, furniture, and electrical tape. Through this definition, students are able to easily identify the functions and expectations of any given area. This clarity is especially important for students with ASD.

Depending on the needs of your students, areas can be more clearly defined by posting visual or text signs. These signs could include such information as when these areas are to be accessed (during free time, group work, etc.), what materials need to stay in the area, and applicable rules.

34. Selecting Student Organizers

Considerations for Selecting Student Organizers

Calendars/Schedules

Checklists

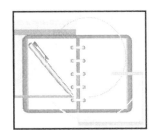
Day Planners

1. What is the purpose of this tool?

2. How will the tool be used?

3. What is the skill level of the student?

4. Is the tool age-appropriate?

5. What type of visuals will support the student (pictures, words, or both)?

6. Is the size of the tool appropriate?

7. Is the tool simple, clear, and concrete?

8. Can the student participate in developing this tool?

9. How will I evaluate whether the tool is working?

Surrey Place Centre, Toronto Region

35. How to Prompt

How to Prompt

Children with PDD can become very prompt dependent. When prompting, it is important to consider the level of prompting required and quickly try to fade prompting. Generally, it is best to prompt from *least* to *most*. In addition, verbal prompting is the hardest to fade, so it is best to consider using other prompting techniques. The following prompts are hierarchical from least to most intrusive:

Least – try these first:
- Gesture
  - o Adult motions the child to respond
  - o Adult points to the task to be initiated (e.g., points to visual schedule)

- Partial physical prompt
  - o Adult provides touch cue such as touching arm, shoulder, elbow to partially assist the initiation (e.g., give elbow a nudge to prompt student to reach for visual schedule)

- Full physical prompt
  - o Adult physically assists the child
  - o Full hand-over-hand prompt

Most – try last:
- Verbal
  - o Adult gives verbal direction (e.g., "Check your schedule.")

Dufferin-Peel Catholic District School Board

36. Prompt Tracking Sheet

PROMPT TRACKING SHEET

INSTRUCTIONS: Staff is to track the number and type of prompts required for the student to complete a task during a specific period of the school day.

TARGET STUDENT: _____

SUBJECT/PERIOD: _____

TASK/TRANSITION	VERBAL PROMPT	PHYSICAL PROMPT F/P (FULL OR PARTIAL)	GESTURE	INDEPENDENT
e.g., silent reading (unfamiliar book)	/	F F P	/	
e.g., computer (preferred activity)				//
TOTAL				

Additional Information:

Halton Catholic District School Board

37. Prompts Used in Initiating Play

Initiating Play Statement

TASK: Initiating Play with a Peer				
• Preparation: two toy trains, train track				
1. Verbal prompt 2. Hand-over-hand prompt 3. Physical prompt 4. Independently	**1**	**2**	**3**	**4**
Walks up to peer who is playing with toy train on track.				
Gets peer's attention.				
Asks, "Can I play with you?"				
Hears response, "Okay."				
Picks up another toy train (not being used by peer).				
Places train on same track.				
Plays with train in shared space.				

TASK:				
• Preparation:				
1. Verbal prompt 2. Hand-over-hand prompt 3. Physical prompt 4. Independently	**1**	**2**	**3**	**4**

Grand Erie District School Board

38. Following Directions

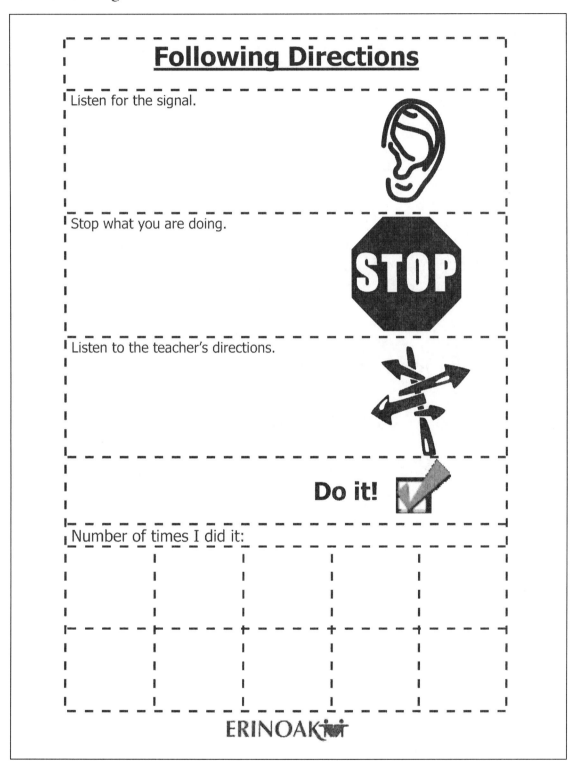

Following Directions

Listen for the signal.

Stop what you are doing.

Listen to the teacher's directions.

Do it!

Number of times I did it:

ERINOAK

39. Interest Inventory

Interest Inventory

Name:

_____

School:

_____

Grade: _____   Age: _____

Favourite food/snack:

Sports you play:

Sports you like to watch:

Favourite subjects at school:

Who do you hang around with?

Games you like to play:

Music:

TV shows that you like to watch:

Computer/Internet:

York Region District School Board

40. Reinforcement Inventory by Parent

Parent/Guardian Reinforcement Inventory

Student's name:_____

Date completed:_____

Completed by:_____

Please check (√) on a scale from 1 to 10.

List what your child is willing to work for.	Least preferred				Somewhat			Most preferred		
	1	2	3	4	5	6	7	8	9	10
Toys and Trinkets 1.										
2.										
3.										
Sports/Physical 1.										
2.										
3.										
Food 1.										
2.										
3.										
Social 1.										
2.										
3.										
Recreation/Entertainment 1.										
2.										
3.										
Community 1.										
2.										
3.										
Domestic 1.										
2.										
3.										
Other reinforcers 1.										
2.										
3.										

See the following page for examples.

(continued)

(continued)

Toys and Trinkets

Balloons, cars, dolls, windup toys, spinning tops, drums, horns, book, pacifier, mirror, fan, plastic bottle filled with coloured water and sparkles, string of beads, squishy balls, elastic putty, silk scarf, computer, stickers, blocks, modelling dough, interlocking building blocks, and so on

Sports/Physical

Flips, twirls, spins (on chairs), tickles, hugs, high-fives, low-fives, pat on the back, jump on a trampoline, piggy back rides, water table, sand table, crawl on the floor, basketball, soccer, skipping, running, and so on

Food

Small candies (jelly beans, etc.), pop, juice, ice cream, frozen treats, cookies, cupcakes, pizza, fruit, veggies, chips, pretzels, popcorn, cereal, french fries, crackers, and so on

Social

Enthusiastic verbal praise, smiles, thumbs-up, applause, wink, sing a song, nod, blow a kiss, raise your arms and shout "Hooray", giggle hysterically, be surprised, helping others (teacher, parent, friend), and so on

Recreation/Entertainment

Watch a video, play a board game, play cards, matching, hide-and-seek, puzzles, colouring, musical chairs, freeze dance, blow bubbles, listen to music, ride a bike, and so on

Community

Go to a movie, go to a restaurant, go shopping, go swimming, visit friends and/or family, go to the park, go for a walk, and so on

Domestic

Baking, cooking, sweeping, wiping tables, washing windows, washing dishes, and so on

York Region District School Board

41. Reinforcement Inventory for Elementary Student

ELEMENTARY STUDENT REINFORCEMENT INVENTORY

Name: _____

School: _____

Grade: _____ Age: _____

1. What are your favourite foods?

   a) _____

   b) _____

   c) _____

2. What do you like to do at recess?

   a) _____

   b) _____

   c) _____

3. What do you like to do at home?

   a) _____

   b) _____

   c) _____

(continued)

(continued)

4. What are your favourite games?

a)_____

b)_____

c)_____

5. What sports do you like to play? _____

6. What sports do you like to watch?_____

7. What are your favourite subjects at school?

a)_____

b)_____

c)_____

8. Who do you like to play with?

a) _____

b) _____

York Region District School Board

42. Giving Praise Effectively

**INCREASING DESIRABLE BEHAVIOUR IN CHILDREN WITH ASD
POSITIVE BEHAVIOURAL STRATEGIES**

Giving Praise Effectively

sitting at circle	"**Wow!** You **sat quietly** during circle!"
I'm ready to work	"**Great!** You are **ready** to do your work!"
colour	"**Beautiful** colouring!"
toys	"Work **finished!** You can choose a toy."

**Praise the completion of each task on
a schedule.
Use descriptive words and focus on the
specific task.
Follow up by rewarding with
preferred activity.**

Durham District School Board

43. Reinforcer Chart

INCREASING DESIRABLE BEHAVIOUR IN CHILDREN WITH ASD POSITIVE BEHAVIOURAL STRATEGIES

I Am Working For

Place picture of reinforcer here

(Represents the number of tokens/stickers to be earned before receiving reward)

Durham District School Board

44. Ten Recommendations

TEN RECOMMENDATIONS FOR WORKING WITH AN AUTISTIC CHILD

Working with an autistic child requires special qualities and skills.

1. Be motivated.

In order to work with an autistic child, you must be highly motivated. In the words of Théo Peeters, *you have to be bitten by the autism bug.*

2. Gather information.

Motivation alone isn't enough. You will need specific training that is both theoretical and practical. Theoretical training will provide an understanding of the fundamental problems related to autism. Practical training will teach you how to implement strategies for working effectively with an autistic child.

Publications, articles, and research findings are an ongoing source of information. Reading works by writers with autism, notably Temple Grandin, Georges Huard, and Gunilla Gerland, will provide insight into the daily lives of people with autism.

3. Gain a new perspective on children with autism.

Forget the myths about autism. Every child is different. It's not because he or she does not WANT to; it's because he or she CAN'T.

4. Think like an autistic child.

As much as you can, think like an autistic child. Question yourself, be flexible, and allow yourself to adapt to the autistic child, without forcing him or her to see the world through your eyes.

5. Adapt the school environment.

The school environment must be adapted to the autistic child so that it provides consistent reference points that make him or her feel safe and increase his or her ability to function autonomously. An autistic child needs an environment that has been adapted to make it easier for him or her to learn and, to the extent possible, make generalizations and open up to the outside world.

(continued)

(continued)

6. Perform appropriate assessments.

In order to create an effective educational program, you must understand the strengths, weaknesses, and interests of the autistic child. In order to do this, you will need evaluation tools that have been adapted for autism, such as the psycho-educational profile. You must use the findings to create a relevant individualized education plan (IEP).

7. Adapt learning to the individual.

Autistic children learn differently. They behave differently. They have different interests. To implement individualized strategies, you must start with the child.

8. Use your imagination.

You must use a lot of imagination in order to meet the needs of an autistic child. You will also need to construct, create, and improvise, using your imagination and a lot of manual dexterity in order to communicate with the child.

9. Cooperate with the school team.

You will need to cooperate very closely with the school staff and the parents. Without them, nothing can be accomplished. You will need to listen to the parents; they are a very important source of information about the child. Cooperation will encourage the sharing of information about difficulties and successes. The well-being of the autistic child and his or her family must always be a central concern.

10. Grow as the autistic child grows.

You must evolve as the autistic child evolves. While remaining vigilant and flexible, you will be constantly learning. Do not settle into a comfortable routine; keep your work with the autistic child dynamic, warm, and lively.

Conseil scolaire de district catholique Centre-Sud

45. Visual Lotto Game

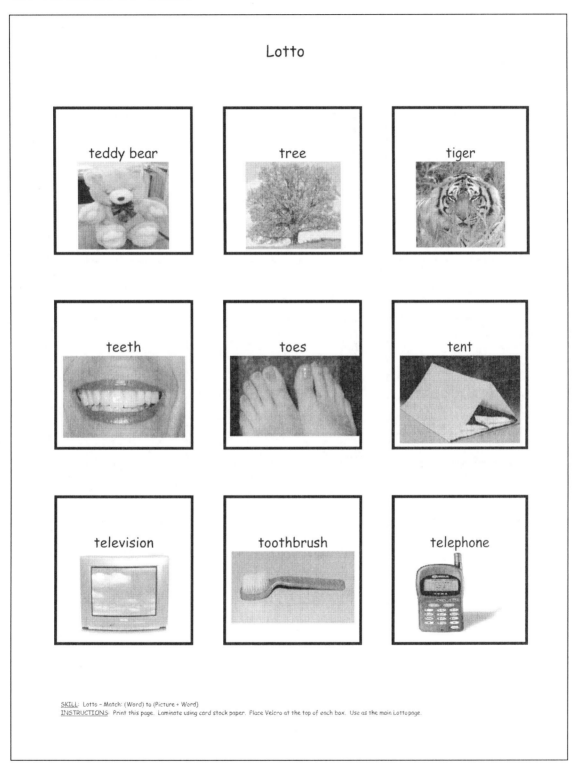

SKILL: Lotto – Match: (Word) to (Picture + Word)
INSTRUCTIONS: Print this page. Laminate using card stock paper. Place Velcro at the top of each box. Use as the main Lotto page.

(continued)

(continued)

Lotto

teddy bear	tree	tiger
teeth	toes	tent
television	toothbrush	telephone

Toronto Catholic District School Board

46. Visual Sentence Strip

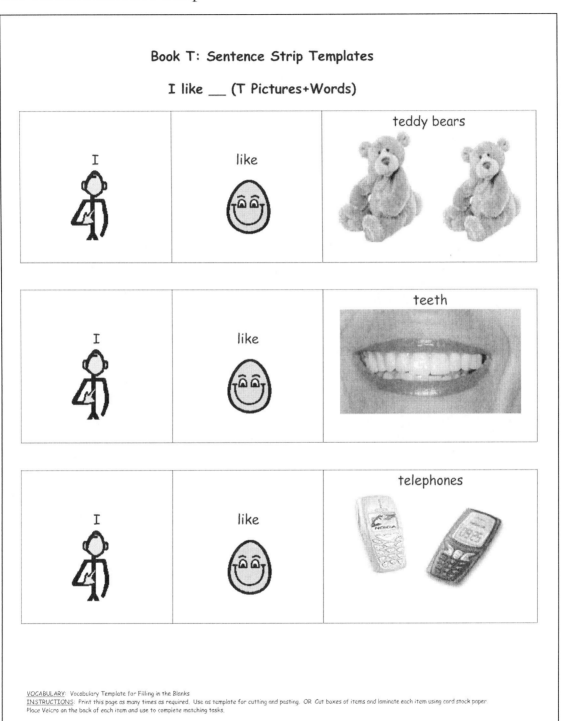

Book T: Sentence Strip Templates

I like ___ (T Pictures+Words)

I	like	teddy bears

I	like	teeth

I	like	telephones

VOCABULARY: Vocabulary Template for Filling in the Blanks
INSTRUCTIONS: Print this page as many times as required. Use as template for cutting and pasting. OR Cut boxes of items and laminate each item using card stock paper. Place Velcro on the back of each item and use to complete matching tasks.

Toronto Catholic District School Board

47. Behavioural Assessments

School Support Program
AUTISM SPECTRUM DISORDER

Behavioural Assessments
Important Information to Record

What to record on the data sheet:

1. A description of the behaviour in observable and measurable terms.

2. The time and date of the incident and the initials of the person recording the behaviour.

3. A description of the onset and ending of the behaviour/occurrence.

4. The setting and surrounding event(s) immediately prior to the occurrence.

5. The details of the response implemented by the caregiver (also known as "the consequence").

Types of Data

- **Frequency (Exact count)**
  Example: frequency of out-of-seat behaviour, number of spitting incidents, number of times the student talked out of turn

- **Duration (Length of time)**
  Example: duration of social interactions; time spent on daily living skills such as mopping, sweeping floors, and setting tables; time spent engaging in inappropriate behaviours such as thumb or finger sucking and behaviours associated with a temper tantrum; amount of time the student was out of his or her seat; time spent completing bathroom routine

Additional Tips

1. When there is a day free of the behaviour, this should be indicated on the data sheet so that other data collectors are aware that data was not missed.

2. When the frequency of the behaviour is high, the data collector can have a second person record the behaviour, choose a time interval to collect data, and choose different time periods throughout the week to collect data. This is considered to be a "time sample" of behaviour.

3. When the frequency of the behaviour is moderate, choose a time interval to collect data, and choose different time periods throughout the week to represent your interval.

4. Remember that the data sheet should be purposeful, relevant, and simple.

Thames Valley Children's Centre

48. Behaviour Tracking Sheet

Behaviour Tracking Sheet

Name: _____   Date: _____

	Period 5			Period 6				Period 7				Home Room	Totals
Appropriate Behaviours	12:00–12:10	12:10–12:20	12:20–12:30	1:40–1:50	1:50–2:00	2:00–2:10	2:10–2:20	2:20–2:30	2:30–2:40	2:40–2:50	2:50–3:00	3:00–3:10	
Saying "hi"													
Approaching someone													
Starting a conversation													
Waiting for a verbal response													
Saying "bye"													
Self-monitoring of swearing													
Totals													
Inappropriate Behaviours													
Interrupting													
Talking out loud/loudly													
Swearing													
Making noises													
Putting hands in pants													
Chinning													
Totals													

√ Check if behaviour observed during time interval

Operational Definitions:

Saying "hi": student independently approaches someone face-to-face and says "hi".

Approaching someone: student approaches someone to try to begin a social interaction.

Starting a conversation: student approaches another person and either asks a question or makes a comment.

Waiting for a verbal response: student independently waits for another person to respond verbally to what he has said before leaving.

Saying "bye": student independently turns to face someone and says "bye" before leaving a social interaction.

Self-monitoring of swearing: student says the initial to middle sounds of a swear word and then stops himself.

Interrupting: student begins to speak at the same time someone else is talking.

Talking out loud/loudly: student suddenly begins speaking out loudly when all is quiet (no one else is talking).

Swearing: student uses vulgar language spontaneously.

Making noises: student suddenly makes unintelligible noises on his own.

Putting hands in pants: student suddenly puts his hands down the back of his pants and keeps them there for more than five seconds.

Chinning: student hits his chin with the palm of his hand more than once.

York Region District School Board

49. Behaviour Frequency Checklist

ASD Resource Team
Behaviour Frequency Checklist

Name:
Dates:
Check = [list behaviour(s), specific, observable, measurable]

Time Period	Monday	Tuesday	Wednesday	Thursday	Friday
1. 8:10 – 8:20 *Entry*					
2. 8:20 – 8:32 *Homeroom*					
3. 8:32 – 9:20					
4. 9:20 – 10:08					
5. 10:08 – 10:56					
6. 10:56 – 11:44					
7. 11:44 – 12:09 *Lunch*					
8. 12:09 – 12:37 *Recess*					
9. 12:37 – 12:44 *Re-Entry*					
10. 12:44 – 1:32					
11. 1:32 – 2:20					
12. 2:20 – 2:35 *Departure*					

Notes:

Peel District School Board

50. ABC Chart

ASD RESOURCE TEAM
FUNCTIONAL BEHAVIOURAL ASSESSMENT: A/B/C CHART

NAME:

DATE	TIME/ LOCATION	What came just before the problem behaviour? ANTECEDENT	Give a full description of the problem BEHAVIOUR	Describe the exact responses to the problem behaviour CONSEQUENCE

Peel District School Board

51. ABC Analysis

ABC Analysis

Date ___ / ___ / ___

Name of the Person Observed: _____

Observer: _____

Behaviours: _____

Date	Time	Antecedent	Behaviour	Consequence	Possible Function

York Region District School Board

52. Functions of Behaviour

Basic Classroom Suggestions Based on Functions of Behaviour

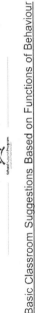

Function	Prevention	Alternative Behaviour (to be taught if appropriate)	Consequence

Attention Seeking	• Identify high-probability times
	• Begin encounters with high rates of attention
	• Change seating arrangement to reduce peer attention
	• Outline classroom expectations AND reinforce with social attending
	• Identify shortest duration student goes without attention-seeking behaviour, then:
	  – schedule positive attention for desired behaviour
	  – systematically fade over time
		• To say "Look at me" or "Watch what I can do"
		• How to tell a joke
		• How to raise hand for teacher's attention
			Redirection:
			• Provide an instruction with guided assistance to ensure correct response, reinforce response with attention, and return to schedule
			• Do not provide any feedback about behaviour

Escape	For the student, provide info for: • What he or she needs to do • How much needs to be done • What will follow the task, etc. For activities, tasks, etc.: • Use reinforcement • Schedule preferred activities between less preferred ones • Use a visual schedule • Provide choice • Shorten duration or decrease size	To request: • An alternative assignment • To do assignment after school • Assistance • Break	Redirection: • Identify contingencies upon returning to assigned area (what work, how much, and what is to follow) • Amend assignment to promote success • Allow temporary escape and reassign once a reinforcer has been identified
Attaining Desired Item	• Reinforce desired behaviour by providing access to desired item • Identify whether absence of desired item will reduce attempts to gain access • Outline when desired item will be available • Provide unlimited access to desired item when satiation is needed • Remember to identify an appropriate replacement item	• To request (e.g., "I want ...") • To name preferred items	Redirection: • Provide instruction for task, then reinforce with desired item • Do not provide access to item after undesirable behaviour occurs • Do not engage in physical battle over item! Instead, regain control of item at first opportunity without physically taking it from student
Meeting Sensory Needs	• Be aware of the student's health issues • Build access to desired activities into daily schedule • Adjust expectations and schedule according to activity level • Assess with OT reinforcers/activities that provide desired sensory wants/needs	• To make general requests • To name sensory toys • To name body parts and feelings (e.g., "I feel sick" card) • To request a break • Relaxation or energizing activity	Redirection: • Provide an instruction with guided assistance to ensure correct response, reinforce response with attention, and return to schedule • Outline when access to preferred activity will be available

Note: This is to assist with developing a behaviour plan that is individualized to a student's needs and based on the results of some form of a functional assessment.

53. Positive Behavioural Intervention Plan

ASD – POSITIVE BEHAVIOURAL INTERVENTION PLAN

Name of Student: Date:
Sex: Grade:
Date of Birth: School:
ASD Resource Team Members:
School-Based Team Members:

Functional Behaviour Assessment/Evaluation Section:

Behaviour(s) in need of change:	Perceived functions of behaviour(s):
1.	1.
2.	2.
3.	3.
Target replacement behaviours:	Hypothesis statement(s):
1.	1.
2.	2.
3.	3.

Strategies to prevent the problem behaviour(s):

1. Strategy 1 and rationale

a)
b)
c)

2. Strategy 2 and rationale

a)
b)
c)

3. Strategy 3 and rationale

a)
b)
c)

Strategies <u>to deal with</u> the problem behaviour(s)

1. Strategy 1 and rationale

a)
b)
c)

2. Strategy 2 and rationale

a)
b)
c)

3. Strategy 3 and rationale

a)
b)
c)

Next review date:

Peel District School Board

54. Communication Observation Form

Communication Observation Form – Requests

Name: _____

Date: _____

Context: _____

Column A = physical manipulation
Column B = giving/showing
Column C = pointing
Column D = gaze shift
Column E = proximity
Column F = head nod/shakes
Column G = facial expressions
Column H = aggression

Column I = tantrum
Column J = crying/whining/screaming
Column K = vocalizing
Column L = verbal (echo)
Column M = verbal (creative)
Column N = other
Column O = other

REQUEST	A	B	C	D	E	F	G	H	I	J	K	L	M	N	O
food/drink															
objects/toys															
action															
help															
permission															
attention															
comfort															
interaction (games, social routines)															
information/questions															
others															

Observations about feelings/emotions:

General observations:

Durham District School Board

55. Checklist for Communication Skills

DEVELOPING COMMUNICATION SKILLS IN PRIMARY-SCHOOL-AGED CHILDREN
WITH AUTISM SPECTRUM DISORDERS

Checklist for Higher-Level Communication Skills

		Never	Sometimes	Often	Always	Not Observed
1	Establishes joint attention					
2	Initiates and responds to greetings					
3	Responds to questions within an appropriate response time					
4	Follows three-step directions without prompts					
5	Understands forms of language (WH– questions, pronouns, word order, possessives, etc.)					
6	Understands classroom routines and adjusts to changes in routines/activities appropriately					
7	Understands non-verbal cues (facial cues, body language, and voice tone changes)					
8	Incorporates non-verbal cues appropriately when communicating					
9	Uses adequate verbal language (with questions, pronouns, word order, possessives, etc.)					
10	Requests clarification/repetition as needed					
11	Responds to the speaker's request for clarification as needed					
12	Understands language used in his/her peer group (jargon, slang)					
13	Uses peer group language					
14	Interrupts appropriately					
15	Gets attention appropriately					
16	Understands jokes/humour					
17	Uses jokes/humour appropriately					
18	Requests permission as needed					
19	Accepts advice/help/reminders appropriately					
20	Requests actions from others appropriately (e.g., asks others to be quiet or stop pushing)					
21	Reacts appropriately when told to change own actions (e.g., be quiet, stop shifting the desk, move)					

(continued)

(continued)

		Never	Sometimes	Often	Always	Not Observed
22	Responds to expressions of affection					
23	Offers expressions of affection					
24	Understands social situations and responds appropriately					
25	Understands apologies appropriately					
26	Uses apologies appropriately					
27	Initiates and ends conversations appropriately					
28	Maintains appropriate body distance/position when conversing					
29	Maintains topics using appropriate verbal/non-verbal skills (uses "Oh", "Mm"; nods)					
30	Takes turns and changes language style appropriately during conversation					
31	Uses appropriate topics during conversations					
32	Tries to repair verbal messages when aware of errors					
33	Presents with a match between verbal and non-verbal message production					
34	Uses language appropriately to agree/disagree with conversational partners					
35	Responds to teasing appropriately					
36	Responds to disappointments appropriately					
37	Follows and gives directions appropriately					
38	Follows and gives reasons for actions and choices appropriately					
39	Communicates verbally with ease and confidence					
40	Other					

2   Durham District School Board

56. Communicative Functions Observation Sheet

Sample Communicative Functions Practice Observations Sheet

Who: _____

Where: _____

When: _____

Additional Information: _____

Function	Example and Tally
Greeting	
Requesting	
Commenting	
Refusing	
Labelling	
Asking questions	
Answering questions	
Joking	
Negotiating	
Other	

York Region District School Board

57. Answering the Telephone

Answering the Telephone

When I am at home, sometimes the phone rings. I can answer it.

I pick up the receiver and say, "Hello".

The person calling will say, "Hello, can I speak to …"

The person will ask to speak to my Mom or Dad.

I answer, "I will get them". I put the receiver on the desk beside the phone and go to get Mom or Dad.

I tell Mom or Dad that someone wants to talk to them on the phone.

Algonquin Child and Family Services, North East Region

58. Social Interaction

Increasing Opportunities for Social Interaction

School Support Program
AUTISM SPECTRUM DISORDER

Student: _____   Month: _____

Time	Routine	Opportunities for Social Interaction	Types of Activities	Who Will Arrange
8:45–9:00	Arrival	Free time at carpet for those ready early	Johnny will bring in a cool toy from home each week to share with others.	Teacher to arrange with family
9:00–9:15	Morning exercises, "O Canada", …	Turn to your right/left, tell your partner one thing you did last night	Johnny is coached at home about the one thing he will talk about, using a picture to remind him.	Johnny's family and classroom staff will develop an inventory of 15 different pictures, and his family will assist Johnny with selecting which one he will do each day and something new he can say.
9:15–9:45	Math	Those who finish early can play a quick game at carpet	Sorting games or games that require matching (e.g., number bingo)	EA will facilitate game to entice others to join.
9:45–10:15	Independent studies	Have a small-group activity for those finished or who are well ahead	Cut and paste, requiring group to decide how to put together	Teacher and EA will alternate facilitating the group.
10:15–10:30	Spelling	Working in pairs	Pairs practise spelling	Johnny is able to pick who his partner will be on alternate days.
10:30–11:00	Science	Small-group experiments	Pictures will be used to allow Johnny to participate in group activity.	Johnny's family will have the experiment sent home so that Johnny can experience and practise answering the questions.

Thames Valley Children's Centre

(continued)

(continued)

Increasing Opportunities for Social Interaction

School Support Program
AUTISM SPECTRUM DISORDERS

Student: _____

Month: _____

Time	Routine	Opportunities for Social Interaction	Types of Activities	Who Will Arrange

Thames Valley Children's Centre

59. Joining a Conversation

JOINING A CONVERSATION

When I want to join a conversation that people are already having,

I should briefly stand nearby to listen to what they are talking about.

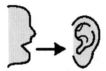

Then I should join in the conversation when I have something to say about what it is they are talking about and there is a break in the conversation.

When joining the conversation, I should;
1. remember NOT to interrupt the person who is already talking; and

2. talk about what everyone else is talking about, NOT what I want to talk about when it is not related to the conversation.
    Topic = school dance
    Topic ≠ dinosaurs

Surrey Place Centre, Toronto Region

60. Activities to Promote Turn Taking

Turn Taking

Turn taking is an important skill for children to learn. It is the beginning of social interaction between the child and another person. Children learn about taking turns in play. Later, children understand taking turns when they speak with others.

Choose games in which the child has to wait for a turn before taking one. You can start by having a really fast turn and then letting him have his turn for longer. Be sure to label with gestures and pointing to let him know whose turn it is, for example, "Your turn" (point to him) and "My turn" (point to yourself). These activities can be tried at home and at school. Remember, having only one item necessitates sharing and taking turns!

Activity	Making It Interactive	Use Words to Label
Ball	Play catch, roll/bounce back and forth, throw ball into a box or pail	ball, throw, bounce, catch
Music (use one drumstick, musical toy)	Take turns hitting the drum, shaking the bell, pushing buttons to activate music	bang, music, drum
Stacking rings	Take turns stacking and removing rings	ring, on, off
Blocks	Build one tower together; take blocks off one at a time	on, block, off, down
Shape sorter	Take turns putting one shape in/taking one shape out	in, out, shape
Craft activities	Use one crayon, one paintbrush, one marker Take turns colouring, painting, etc.	on, colour, paint
Doll and accessories	Take turns with one doll, one brush, one spoon, one bottle, etc.	brush, eat, hug, dolly, eat, drink, bottle, milk
Cars/trucks	Take turns driving one car down a ramp, along a road	car, drive, on, down
Sand play	Take turns using toys in the sand: one shovel, one strainer, one pail, one scoop	in, sand, shovel, pail, pour

Halton Catholic District School Board

61. Prompts Used in Turn Taking

My turn.

Your turn.

Turn Taking

Initally, adult to child.
Adult selects activity that student enjoys.
Activity: Modelling dough

	Hand over hand	Verbal/ Physical prompts	Physical Prompts	Independ- ently
1. Gets modelling dough				
2. Brings to desk				
3. Opens container				
4. Takes out modelling dough and tools				
5. Places bin on floor beside desk; teacher says, "My turn"				
6. Takes modelling dough				
7. Rolls modelling dough; after a few minutes, teacher says, "My turn"				
8. Hands tools and modelling dough to teacher				
9. Waits several minutes; teacher says, "Your turn"				
REPEAT PROCESS 3 OR 4 TIMES				
10. Picks up bin				
11. Places it on desk				
12. Helps teacher place items in bin				
13. Returns bin to shelf				

Halton Catholic District School Board

62. Play Checklist

Play Checklist

Name:	Date:

In what type of play activity does your student engage?
- ☐ Plays alone
- ☐ Observes peers playing
- ☐ Imitates peer play
- ☐ Parallel play
- ☐ Adult-directed peer play
- ☐ Plays with another student
- ☐ Plays with a group of students
- ☐ Seeks out play partner
- ☐ Interacts only with primary caregiver

How does your student play/use toys?
- ☐ To explore
- ☐ For self-stimulation
- ☐ For sensory stimulation
- ☐ To experience cause and effect
- ☐ Plays with the same toy all the time
- ☐ Indicates interest in simple toys
- ☐ Uses simple toys incorrectly
- ☐ Uses simple toys correctly

Describe your student's social communication skills during play.
- ☐ Initiates play
- ☐ Shares materials with direction
- ☐ Shares materials independently
- ☐ Resists intrusion
- ☐ Tolerates intrusion

Describe your student's social turn-taking skills.
- ☐ Takes turns with direction
- ☐ Take turns independently

How does your student focus during play?
- ☐ Demonstrates the capacity for joint attention
- ☐ Shifts from one toy to the next frequently
- ☐ Requires constant adult support
- ☐ Requires occasional adult support
- ☐ Is disruptive
- ☐ Operates independently

Durham District School Board

63. Fitness Friends Program

Fitness Friends

The Fitness Friends program was developed cooperatively by the Durham Catholic District School Board, the Durham District School Board, EMT – Energize, Motivate, Train, and Variety Village. This free program is designed to encourage students of all abilities to get involved in sports and be active.

Schools enter as many teams as they wish, with each team consisting of one student with a disability, one peer, and a staff member. Teams participate in as many sport and recreational activities as possible within a specified time period (e.g., 10–12 weeks). Teams record and submit the type and duration of activities to earn Fitness Friends points.

A monthly Fitness Friends newsletter is distributed to highlight success stories submitted by teams, fitness tips, nutrition facts, and other active-living ideas. Achievements of all of the participants are celebrated with a region-wide Fitness Friends Festival at the end of the program.

Objectives

The Fitness Friends program aims to promote an active lifestyle, especially for students with a disability, and increase opportunities for students to participate in sports and recreation activities outside the school curriculum and physical education classes.

The program encourages students of all abilities to:
- Participate in inclusive sport and recreation activities
- Embrace ability, diversity, inclusion, and physical fitness
- Focus on friendship, everyone's ability, and personal achievement

The program further provides:
- Resources for adapted equipment and adapted programs to support physical activity, health, and nutrition
- Recognition for participation and a venue for celebrating everyone's achievements

Activity Examples

Walk/Jog/Wheel	Floor Hockey/Sledge	Tai Chi
Simon Says	Hockey	Stretching
Relay	Obstacle Course	Target Games
Baseball	Hiking	Swimming

Activity Recording Example

Date	Activity	Duration of Activity	Points to Date	Staff Initial
Feb. 8	Walk/wheel	20 minutes	20	CH
Feb. 10	Relay	30 minutes	50	CH
Feb. 13	Target games	15 minutes	65	CH

Durham Catholic District School Board

64. Integrated Games Group

**Conseil des
écoles publiques
de l'Est de l'Ontario**

Date: _____

Dear parents or guardians,

My name is (team member). I work in the special education department of Education Services on the team providing specialized interventions for children with an Autism Spectrum Disorder. This year, the special education department wants to set up a pilot project for integrated games groups. The project will run at (name of school) public elementary school.

Your child has been selected to take part as a "novice player" in the integrated games groups program. This program is intended to develop communication and social skills through game playing. The objective of this program is to encourage children to learn to play in a functional manner while having fun with the other children in their group. The novice player also has a model, called the "expert player", so that he or she can imitate the skills required to interact with another person.

I would like to invite your child to take part in the games groups with three children from his or her class. This play group will be held twice a week for 30 to 40 minutes a session.

If you agree to have your child take part in the integrated games groups, please sign below. If you have any questions or if you would like further information about the games groups, you can contact me at _____ , or you can contact the principal at _____.

Thank you for your cooperation,

(team member)

Parents' signature _____

Adapted from a letter published in *Peer Play and the Autism Spectrum: The Art of Guilding Children's Socialization and Imagination*, by Pamela J. Wolfberg (2003).

Conseil des écoles publiques de l'Est de l'Ontario

Integrated Games Groups

| Participant Sheet |

Student's name:

Date:

Theme:

<u>Objective(s):</u>

Objective(s):	Observation(s):
1-	
2-	
3-	

Conseil des écoles publiques de l'Est de l'Ontario

65. Social Scenario

**Conseil des
écoles publiques
de l'Est de l'Ontario**

**Education Services
Special Education Department**

Social Scenario

A social scenario helps an autistic student to learn the underlying rules of social exchanges or interactions and to choose the behaviour that is desirable in a social situation.

In a social scenario, the adult describes to the child in detail the way he or she should behave, explaining what is expected in the particular situation, and telling the student that if he/she behaves in this way, the adult will be proud of the child and the adults around him/her will be pleased.

The adult can read the story to the student or the student can read it him/herself. It is suggested that the story be read at least twice a day for at least three weeks. For example, if the student is having problems in the schoolyard, the teacher will read the story to the child before he/she goes out for recess and then read it again after recess.

We believe that it is very important to personalize the story so that it is related to each student's emotional experiences, because each child is unique.

A social scenario helps a student reduce his/her level of anxiety because he/she knows what is expected in the environment when faced with a particular social situation.

Everybody Makes Mistakes

Students are tested in the classroom. There are tests for mathematics, French, English, science, and so on.

A test tells a student whether or not he or she has clearly understood what the teacher has shown him/her.

If he/she has clearly understood, the student may do very well on the test.

Sometimes, if he/she has not understood as well, the student may make mistakes in his/her test. It is normal to make mistakes. All students make mistakes. When we are learning, we make mistakes. The teacher will help the student to understand clearly.

I sometimes do very well on a test. But sometimes I make mistakes in my test. It is normal for me to make mistakes. I make mistakes because I am learning. This is not serious; the teacher will help me to understand clearly and to correct my mistakes.

I am proud that I can correct my mistakes when I have a test.

The adult is pleased that I correct my mistakes when I have a test.

Conseil des écoles publiques de l'Est de l'Ontario

66. My Morning Routine

My Morning Routine

I come to school on the school bus.

I play in the school yard with my friends.

I go to my locker. I hang up my coat, I change my shoes,

and I get my agenda.

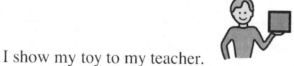

I show my toy to my teacher. I tell her why I brought it to school.

I put my toy in the box. I can play with it at recess time.

I am ready to work.

Pathways for Children and Youth, South East Region

67. Steps to Reading Body Language

Steps to ...

Reading Body Language

1   Look for clues:
   a) the face
   b) gestures
   c) what the body does

2   Recognize the clue.

3   Understand the clue.

4   Respond to the clue.

Kinark Child and Family Services, Central East Region

68. Body and Facial Expressions

Directions: Cut each row out and place in a jar or envelope. Ask a student to take a paper from the jar and act out the body and facial gestures; have the other students guess what the student is feeling.

Body and Facial Gestures	Feeling
You have a bad stomachache. Hold your stomach, bend over, and look like you are in pain.	In pain
You have lost your book report. Look worried.	Worried
You hear a loud noise behind you. Turn around and look afraid.	Afraid
Your team won. Jump up and down. Clap your hands and look excited.	Excited
Your homework is too hard. Look frustrated.	Frustrated
Your parents brought you a present when they returned from a trip. Look surprised.	Surprised
The movie is boring. Turn away and look bored.	Bored
Your team lost the race. Hang your head down and look sad.	Sad
Your teacher has given you two spelling lists. You don't know which one to study. Look confused.	Confused
You won a prize. Stand up straight and look happy.	Happy
You tore your favourite sweatshirt. Look upset.	Upset

Kinark Child and Family Services, Central East Region

69. Different Kinds of Touch

There Are Different Kinds of Touch

When I am with other people that I know, there are some kinds of touch that are okay and some that are not okay.

When I am with my family, it is okay to hug them.

When I am with my friends, it is okay to do high-fives.

When I am with teachers, it is okay to shake hands.

It is never okay to touch other people on their private areas.

It is not okay to hug or kiss other students or teachers at school.

Surrey Place Centre, Toronto Region

70. Public/Private Places

Public/Private Places

Public	Private
Define what public *means* A public place is:	*Define what* private *means* A private place is:
List all the public places you can think of:	List private places: Bedroom at home Bathroom at home
List all the things you can do in public:	List all the things you can do in private:

Pathways for Children and Youth, South East Region

71. Tips for Job Coaches

Tips for Coaching Students with an ASD to Be Successful in the Workforce

When coaching students with an Autism Spectrum Disorder (ASD) to find employment and be successful in the workplace, the main goal of the job coach is to teach the employee to work independently and to no longer require support in order to achieve success. To make this happen, the job coach must ensure that the person with an ASD

understands the requirements of the position, and educate the employer and co-workers about the strengths and needs of the individual with an ASD. Once these goals have been reached, a good job coach will then phase him/herself out through the creation of natural supports so the employee learns to advocate for him/herself and is able to work independently.

ERINOAK

Coach the Employee

The job coach paves the way for success by helping the employee to understand the expectations of the role and by ensuring that he/she understands what the responsibility will be. The job coach also helps to break each job responsibility down into manageable "chunks" so that the employee is able to work through each step in a systematic manner. The job coach also helps to ensure success by facilitating communication between the employer and the employee, ensuring that the employer addresses the employee in an effective manner.

Support and Educate the Employer

It is the role of the job coach to prepare the employer and co-workers for working with an individual with an ASD. It is important that the employer understand the special requirements of the person with an ASD, specifically how to communicate effectively. The employer should also be provided with tips such as these:

• Instructions should be direct and broken down into manageable steps that can be completed systematically. Students with an ASD often struggle with multitasking, so job expectations should reflect their need for a step-by-step sequence.

• Students with an ASD work best when their routine is consistent. For example, they may need to work at the same workstation and have breaks at the same time.

• If required to make decisions or problem-solve, the person with an ASD may require examples of the type of answer expected.

Phase Out Support

Too much support and too little support can both result in frustration on the part of the employer and the employee. To ensure success once the job coach moves off-site, s/he needs to create *natural supports* to take on the role. For example, identify two or three co-workers who can serve as mentors. The job coach should do this, as

students with an ASD often struggle to build relationships. Employees must also realize that they cannot rely too heavily on this mentor. The job coach should also teach the protocol of the office: who to ask questions of, who to call when ill, etc.

72. Stress Thermometer

Stress Thermometer

Stress Signals

Relaxation Techniques

6

5

4

3

2

1

Feeling Good

McMaster Children's Hospital, Hamilton/Niagara Region

73. Relaxation Steps

CHEO Children's Hospital of Eastern Ontario
Centre hospitalier pour enfants de l'est de l'Ontario

Relaxation Steps

1. Move to the quiet place.

2. Sit on a chair, beanbag, or on the floor.

3. Think about a place that is relaxing for you.

4. Breathe slowly and steadily.   1 2 3 4 5

5. Tense shoulders up,   1 2 3 4 5
   relax shoulders down.

6. Tense hands, relax hands.   1 2 3 4 5

7. Tense toes, relax toes.   1 2 3 4 5

8. Breathe slowly and steadily.   1 2 3 4 5

Finished !

Children's Hospital of Eastern Ontario, Eastern Region

74. Study Tips for Teens

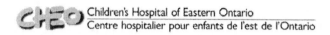

Children's Hospital of Eastern Ontario
Centre hospitalier pour enfants de l'est de l'Ontario

autism
autisme

Tips for When the Teacher Talks

➤ **Listen carefully during class.**

➤ **If you feel you are getting distracted, you can ask for a study carrel, ask for a different seat, ...**

➤ **Ask the teacher if you can use a tape recorder.**

➤ **Listen for some cues like "This is important", "This will probably be on the test", "The main point is ...".**

Tips for Taking Notes

➤ **Write headings or titles for each new topic. You will know when it is a new topic because the teacher might say, "We are going to be doing [*insert new topic here*] now".**

➤ **Use bullet points for ideas that relate to one topic. For example:**

> North Pole:
> ◊ No land
> ◊ Slabs of ice
> ◊ Very cold
> ◊ Six months of daylight and six months of darkness

➤ **Leave some empty space. Leave line spaces between points.**

➤ **Ask a classmate to lend you his or her notes.**

Tips for Organization

➤ **Try to keep all your pens, pencils, and other school supplies in a pencil case; the best kind is one that can fit into your three-ring binder.**

➤ **Get one binder for each subject. Each binder should be a different colour, for example, red for history, blue for science, ...**

APPENDICES

IN THE APPENDICES

Appendix A: Glossary   208

Appendix B: Resources   209

Appendix C: References   211

Appendix A: Glossary

Accommodations
Special teaching and assessment strategies, human supports, and/or individualized equipment required to enable a student to learn and demonstrate learning. Accommodations do not alter the provincial curriculum expectations for the grade.

Alternative expectations
Learning expectations that are developed to help students acquire knowledge and skills that are not represented in the Ontario curriculum

Assistive technology
Any technology that allows one to increase, maintain, or improve the functional capabilities of an individual with special learning needs (Edyburn, 2000)

Augmentative and Alternative Communication (AAC)
Communication that makes use of services and devices, such as visual symbols, signs, or voice output devices, to supplement (augment) or replace (serve as an alternative to) a student's current method of communication

Autism Spectrum Disorders (ASD)
A subset of the Pervasive Developmental Disorders (PDDs) that includes Autistic Disorder, PDD NOS, and Asperger's Disorder. These disorders have three areas of concern:
- Qualitative impairments in social skills
- Qualitative impairments in verbal and non-verbal communication
- Restricted and repetitive interests or behaviours.

Collaboration
Planning, implementing, shared decision-making, and working together to provide services (Minister's Autism Spectrum Disorders Reference Group, 2007)

Comorbid disorders
Two or more disorders diagnosed simultaneously in an individual

Echolalia
Repetition of words or phrases used by others

Functional behaviour assessment (FBA)
A systematic process that is designed to look beyond the student's behaviour and focus on identifying its function or purpose

Functional analysis
A systematic process to develop or confirm a hypothesis about the function of behaviour

Modified expectations
Learning expectations that differ in some way from the regular grade expectations as outlined in the Ministry of Education's curriculum policy documents

Splinter skills
Highly developed skills in a very specific area of ability

Transition planning
A coordinated set of activities that prepare students for change (Ministers' Autism Spectrum Disorders Reference Group, 2007)

Appendix B: Resources

Websites for Information and Resources on ASD

ABA Resources www.abaresources.com

Ability OnLine www.ablelink.org

Alberta Teachers' Association – Behaviour, Observation, Assessment and Teaching Strategies (BOATS) www.specialeducation.ab.ca/

A Rhyme a Week: Nursery Rhymes for Early Literacy http://curry.edschool.virginia.edu/go/wil/rimes_and_rhymes.htm

ASD: Canadian-American Research Consortium www.autismresearch.ca

Asperger Society Ontario www.aspergers.ca

Autism Ontario www.autismontario.com

Autism Research Institute www.autism.com/ari

Autism Society Canada www.autismsocietycanada.ca/

Autisme Montréal www.autisme-montreal.com

AutismToday www.autismtoday.com

Canadian Autism Intervention Research Network (CAIRN) www.cairn-site.com

ConnectAbility www.connectability.ca

Do2Learn www.do2learn.org

Geneva Centre for Autism www.autism.net/index.php

Indiana Resource Center for Autism (IRCA) www.iidc.indiana.edu/~irca/welcome2.html

International Rett Syndrome Association www.rettsyndrome.org

Ministry of Children and Youth Services www.children.gov.on.ca

Picture Communication Symbols http://mayer-johnson.com/Downloads.aspx

Online Asperger Syndrome Information and Support (O.A.S.I.S.) www.udel.edu/bkirby/asperger/

Sensory Resources www.sensoryresources.com

Société québécoise de l'autisme www.autisme.qc.ca

Special Needs Opportunity Window http://snow.utoronto.ca/

Temple Grandin – Teaching Tips for Children and Adults with Autism www.autism.org//temple/tips.html

The Gray Center for Social Learning & Understanding www.thegraycenter.org

Children's Books on ASD

Amenta, Charles A. III (1992). *Russell Is Extra Special: A Book About Autism for Children.* Magination Press. The story of an autistic boy and his family who help children and adults understand this developmental disorder.

Band, Eve B., Hecht, Emily, & Cotton, Sue Lynn (2001). *Autism Through a Sister's Eyes: A Book for Children About High-Functioning Autism and Related Disorders.* Future Horizons. Ten-year-old Emily explains her feelings and her search for answers about why her brother Daniel did the things he did.

Bishop, Beverly (2003). *My Friend with Autism: A Coloring Book for Peers and Siblings.* Future Horizons.

Edwards, Becky (1999). *My Brother Sammy.* Bloomsbury Publishing. Sammy's older brother learns that Sammy's way of doing things may not be so bad.

Haddon, Mark (2004). *The Curious Incident of the Dog in the Night-Time.* Anchor Canada. Fifteen-year-old Christopher has a condition similar to autism and does not like to be touched, meet new people, or make small talk. When his neighbour's dog is killed, Christopher begins an investigation that disrupts his perfectly ordered life.

Hoopmann, Kathy (2000). *Blue Bottle Mystery: An Asperger Adventure.* Jessica Kingsley Publishers. A fantasy story about an adventure with a mysterious old bottle Ben, who has Asperger's Syndrome, and his friend Andy find in the schoolyard.

Lears, Laurie (1997). *Ian's Walk: A Story About Autism.* Albert Whitman & Company. A story about a girl who realizes how much her little brother, who has autism, means to her as she searches for him when he is lost.

Messner, Abby Ward (1996). *Captain Tommy.* Potential Unlimited Publishing. A story about a young boy who at first reluctantly agrees to play with and then makes friends with a boy who has PDD.

Murrell, Diane (2001). *Tobin Learns to Make Friends.* Future Horizons. A picture book about Tobin, a train that learns to make friends and engage in proper social activities.

Ogaz, Nancy (2002). *Buster and the Amazing Daisy.* Jessica Kingsley Publishers. A fictional story about Daisy, who faces new challenges and makes new friends when she joins a mainstream class and trains Buster the rabbit for a pet show.

Thompson, Mary (1996). *Andy and His Yellow Frisbee.* Woodbine House. The new girl at school tries to befriend Andy, an autistic boy who spends every recess by himself spinning a yellow Frisbee under the watchful eye of his older sister.

Watson, Esther (1996). *Talking to Angels.* Harcourt Brace. A non-fiction book about the author's autistic sister.

Welton, Jude (2005). *Adam's Alternative Sports Day: An Asperger Story.* Jessica Kingsley Publishers. A nine-year-old child with Asperger's Syndrome copes with the everyday challenges of school.

Appendix C: References

Adams, J.I. (1995). *Autism – PDD: Introducing strategies for parents and professionals.* Kent Bridge, ON: Adams Publications.

Alberta Learning (2003). *Teaching students with Autism Spectrum Disorders.* Edmonton, AB: Alberta Learning.

Alberto, P.A., & Troutman, A.C. (2006). *Applied Behaviour Analysis for teachers.* Upper Saddle River, N.J.: Pearson Prentice Hall.

Allen, D.A. (1988). Autistic spectrum disorders: Clinical presentation in preschool children. *Journal of Child Neurology*, Vol. 3, pp. 48–56.

American Psychiatric Association (APA) (2000). *Diagnostic and statistical manual of mental disorders–IV Text revision (DSM-IV-TR).* Washington, D.C.: American Psychiatric Association.

American Psychiatric Association (APA) (1994). *Diagnostic and statistical manual of mental disorders–IV (DSM-IV).* Washington, D.C.: American Psychiatric Association.

American Psychiatric Association (APA) (1980). *Diagnostic and statistical manual of mental disorders–III (DSM-III).* Washington, D.C.: American Psychiatric Association.

Attwood, T. (2007). *The complete guide to Asperger's Syndrome.* London, U.K.: Jessica Kingsley Publishers.

Autism Genome Project Consortium (2007). Mapping autism risk loci using genetic linkage and chromosomal rearrangements. *Nature Genetics*, Vol. 39, No. 3, pp. 319–328.

Autism Society Ontario (2002). *Navigating the special education system in Ontario – A handbook for parents of children with Autism Spectrum Disorders.* Toronto: Autism Society Ontario.

Barnard, J., Harvey, V., Potter, D., & Prior, A. (2001). *Ignored or ineligible? The reality for adults with Autism Spectrum Disorders.* London: The National Autistic Society.

Bauer, S. Asperger Syndrome, *Online Asperger Syndrome Information and Support*, www.udel.edu/bkirby/asperger/as_thru_years.html.

Bellini, S. (2003). Making (and keeping) friends: A model for social skills instruction. *IRCA Reporter*, Vol. 8, No. 3, pp. 1–10.

Bellini, S., & Akullian, J. (2007). A meta-analysis of video modeling and video self-modeling interventions for children and adolescents with Autism Spectrum Disorders. *Exceptional Children*, Vol. 73, No. 3, pp. 264–287.

Biederman, G.B., Fairhall, J.L., Raven, K.A., & Davey, V.A. (1998). Verbal prompting, hand-over-hand instruction, and passive observation in teaching children with developmental disabilities. *Exceptional Children*, Vol. 64, No. 4, pp. 503–511.

Blischak, D.M., & Schlosser, R.W. (2003). Use of technology to support independent spelling by students with autism. *Topics in Language Disorders*, Vol. 23, pp. 293–304.

Brannon, E. (2005). The independence of language and mathematical reasoning. *Proceedings of the National Academy of Science*, Vol. 102, No. 9.

British Columbia Ministry of Education (2000). *Teaching students with autism: A resource guide for schools.* British Columbia Ministry of Education.

Broun, L.T. (2004). Teaching students with Autism Spectrum Disorders to read: A visual approach. *Teaching Exceptional Children,* Vol. 36, No. 4, pp. 36–40.

Bryson, S.D. (1996). Brief reports: Epidemiology of autism. *Journal of Autism and Developmental Disorders,* Vol. 26, pp. 25–35.

Buckley, S.D., & Newchok, D.K. (2004) Differentiated impact of response effort within response chain on use of mands in a student with autism. *Research in Developmental Disabilities,* Vol. 26, pp. 77–86.

Chakrabarti, S., & Fombonne, E. (2005) Pervasive developmental disorders in preschool children: Confirmation of high prevalence. *American Journal of Psychiatry,* Vol. 162, pp. 1133–1141.

Coffey, K.M., & Obringer, S.J. (2004). A case study on autism: School accommodations and inclusive settings. *Education,* Vol. 124, No. 4, pp. 632–639.

Dalrymple, N.J. (1995). Environmental supports to develop flexibility and independence. In K.A. Quill (Ed.), *Teaching children with autism: Strategies to enhance communication and socialization.* Albany, NY: Delmar.

Delano, M., & Snell, M.E., The effects of social stories on the social engagement of children with autism. *Journal of Positive Behavior Interventions,* Vol. 8, No. 1, Winter 2006, pp. 29–42.

DiSalvo, C.A., & Oswald, D.P. Peer-mediated interventions to increase the social interaction of children with autism: Consideration of peer expectancies. *Focus on Autism and Other Developmental Disabilities,* Vol. 17, No. 4, Winter 2002.

Durand, V.M., & Merges, E. (2001). Functional communication training: A contemporary behavior analytic intervention for problem behaviors. *Focus on Autism and Other Developmental Disorders,* Vol. 16, pp. 110–119.

Edyburn, D.L. (2000). Assistive technology and students with mild disabilities. *Focus on Exceptional Children,* Vol. 32, No. 9, pp. 1–24.

Fombonne, E. (2003). Epidemiological surveys of autism and other pervasive developmental disorders: An update. *Journal of Autism and Developmental Disorders,* Vol. 33, No. 4, pp. 365–382.

Fombonne, E., Zakarian, R., Bennett, A., Meng, L., & McLean-Heywood, D. (2006). Pervasive developmental disorders in Montreal, Quebec, Canada: Prevalence and links with immunizations. *Pediatrics,* Vol. 118, No. 1, pp. 139–150.

Geneva Centre for Autism
www.autism.net/index.php

Grandin, T. (2007). Autism from the inside. *Educational Leadership,* Vol. 64, No. 5, pp. 29–32.

Grandin, T. (1995). *Thinking in Pictures.* New York: Doubleday.

Gresham, F.M. (1995). Best practices in social skills training. In A. Thomas and J. Grimes, (Eds.), *Best practices in school psychology.* Washington, DC: National Association of School Psychologists.

Harris, S.L. (2004). Autism intervention. In Centre of Excellence for Early Childhood Development (CEECD), *Encyclopedia on early childhood development.* Published online July 8, 2004. www.excellence-earlychildhood.ca/documents/HarrisANGxp.pdf

Heflin, L.J., & Alaimo, D.F. (2007). *Students with Autism Spectrum Disorders: Effective instructional practices.* Upper Saddle River, N.J.: Pearson Prentice Hall.

Higgins, D.J., Bailey, S.R., & Pearce, J.C. (2005). Factors associated with functioning style and coping strategies of families with a child with an autism spectrum disorder. *Sage Publications and the National Autistic Society*, Vol. 9, No. 2, pp. 125–137.

Hodgdon, L.A. (1999). *Solving behavior problems in autism*. Troy, MI: QuickRoberts Publishing.

Howlin, P. (1998). Practitioner review: Psychological and educational treatments for autism. *Journal of Child Psychology and Psychiatry and Allied Disciplines*, Vol. 39, No. 3, pp. 307–322.

Iovannone, R., Dunlap, G., Huber, H., & Kincaid, D. (2003). Effective educational practices for students with Autism Spectrum Disorders. *Focus on Autism and Other Developmental Disabilities*, Vol. 18, No. 3, Fall, pp. 150–165.

Jackson, L. (2002). *Freaks, geeks and Asperger Syndrome*. London, U.K.: Jessica Kingsley Publishers.

Judge, S.L. (2001). Computer applications in programs for young children with disabilities: Current status and future directions. *Journal of Special Education Technology*, Vol. 16, No. 1, pp. 29–40.

Kanner, L. (1943). Autistic disturbances of affective contact. *Nervous Child*, Vol. 2, pp. 217–250.

Kluth, P. (2003). *You're going to love this kid: Teaching students with autism in the inclusive classroom*. Baltimore, MD: Paul H. Brooks Publishing.

Lawson, W. (1998). *Life behind glass: A personal account of Autism Spectrum Disorder*. London, U.K.: Jessica Kingsley Publishers.

Layton, T.L., & Watson, L.R. (1995). Enhancing communication in nonverbal children with autism. In K.A. Quill (Ed.), *Teaching children with autism: Strategies to enhance communication and socialization*. Albany, NY: Delmar.

Manitoba Education, Citizenship and Youth (2005). *Supporting inclusive schools: A handbook for developing and implementing programming for students with Autism Spectrum Disorder*. Winnipeg: Manitoba Education, Citizenship and Youth.

Ministers' Autism Spectrum Disorders Reference Group (2007). *Making a difference for students with Autism Spectrum Disorders in Ontario schools: From evidence to action*. Toronto: Queen's Printer for Ontario.

Mirenda, P. (2003). He's not really a reader ... Perspectives on supporting literacy development in individuals with autism. *Topics in Language Disorders*, Vol. 23, pp. 271–282.

Myles, B.S., & Simpson, R.L. (1998). *Asperger Syndrome: A guide for educators and parents*. Austin, TX: PRO-ED.

National Research Council (2001). *Educating children with autism*. Committee on Educational Interventions for Children with Autism. Catherine Lord and James P. McGee (Eds.). Division of Behavioral and Social Sciences and Education. Washington, D.C.: National Academy Press.

New Brunswick Department of Education (2005). *Teaching students with Autism Spectrum Disorders*, pp. 47–48. Fredericton: New Brunswick Department of Education.

Olley, J.G. (1999). Curriculum for students with autism. *School Psychology Review*, Vol. 28, pp. 595–607.

Ontario Ministry of Education (2007a). Policy/Program Memorandum No. 140, Incorporating methods of Applied Behaviour Analysis (ABA) into programs for students with Autism Spectrum Disorders (ASD). Toronto: Ontario Ministry of Education.

Ontario Ministry of Education (2007b). *Special education funding guidelines: Special Equipment Amount (SEA) and Special Incidence Portion (SIP), 2007–08.* Toronto: Ontario Ministry of Education.

Ontario Ministry of Education (2005a). *Education for all: The report of the Expert Panel on Literacy and Numeracy Instruction for Students With Special Education Needs, Kindergarten to Grade 6.* Toronto: Ontario Ministry of Education.

Ontario Ministry of Education (2005b). *Planning entry to school: A resource guide.* Toronto: Ontario Ministry of Education.

Ontario Ministry of Education (2004). *The Individual Education Plan (IEP): A resource guide.* Toronto: Ontario Ministry of Education.

Ontario Ministry of Education (2002). *Transition planning: A resource guide.* Toronto: Ontario Ministry of Education.

Ontario Ministry of Education (2001). *Special education: A guide for educators.* Toronto: Ontario Ministry of Education.

Ontario Ministry of Education (2000). *Individual Education Plans: Standards for development, program planning, and implementation.* Toronto: Ontario Ministry of Education.

Ontario Ministry of Education (1982). Policy/Program Memorandum No. 11, Early identification of children's learning needs. Toronto: Ontario Ministry of Education.

Ontario Regulation 181/98, Identification and placement of exceptional pupils. Regulation made under the Education Act. www.e-laws.gov.on.ca/DBLaws/Statutes.

Parsons, S., & Mitchell, P. (2002). The potential of virtual reality in social skills training for people with autistic spectrum disorders. *Journal of Intellectual Disability Research*, Vol. 46, No. 5, pp. 430–443.

Perry, A., & Condillac, R. (2003). *Evidence-based practices for children and adolescents with Autism Spectrum Disorders: Review of the literature and practice guide.* Toronto: Children's Mental Health Ontario.

Quill, K.A. (Ed.). (1995). *Teaching children with autism: Strategies to enhance communication and socialization.* Albany, NY: Delmar.

Randle, K. (2005). *A research study investigating the use of assistive technology with students in British Columbia.* Special Education Technology – British Columbia (SET-BC) website, March 2007.

Richard, G.J. (1997). *The source for autism.* East Moline, IL: LinguiSystems, Inc.

Rydell, P.J., & Prizant, B.M. (1995). Assessment and intervention strategies for children who use echolalia. In K.A. Quill (Ed.), *Teaching children with autism: Strategies to enhance communication and socialization.* Albany, NY: Delmar.

Saskatchewan Education (1999). *Teaching students with autism: A guide for educators,* pp. 32–33. Saskatchewan Education.

Saulnier, C.A., Klin, A., Sparrow, S.S., Cicchetti, D.V., Volkmar, F.R., & Lord, C. (York Child Study Center). (2006). Does high IQ in Autism Spectrum Disorders translate into real-life success? *Materials of the 5th Annual International Meeting for Autism Research (IMFAR),* p. 40.

Simpson, R.L. (2007). Issues, trends, and scientifically-based practices for learners with Asperger Disorder. *Progress and challenges in the behavioral treatment of autism,* Association for Behavioral Analysis International, February 2–4, 2007.

Szatmari, P., Jones, M.B., Zwaigenbaum, L., & MacLean, J.E. (1998). Genetics of autism: Overview and new directions. *Journal of Autism and Developmental Disorders*, Vol. 28, No. 5, pp. 351–368.

Tanguay, P.B. (2002). *Nonverbal learning disabilities at school: Educating students with NLD, Asperger Syndrome, and related conditions.* London: Jessica Kingsley Publishers.

Twachtman, D.D. (1995). Methods to enhance communication in verbal children. In K.A. Quill (Ed.), *Teaching children with autism: Strategies to enhance communication and socialization.* Albany, NY: Delmar.

Weber, K., & Bennett, S. (2004). *Special education in Ontario schools* (5th ed.). Palgrave, ON: Highland Press.

Welton, E., Vakil, S., & Carasea, C. (2004). Strategies for increasing positive social interactions in children with autism: A case study. In *Teaching Exceptional Children*, Vol. 37, No. 1, Sept./Oct., p. 45.

Williams White, S., Scahill, L., Klin, A., Koenig, K., & Volkmar, F.R. (2006). Educational placements and service use patterns of individuals with Autism Spectrum Disorders. *Journal of Autism and Developmental Disorders*, November.

Wing, L. (1988). The continuum of autistic disorders. In E. Schopler & G.M. Mesibov (Eds.), *Diagnosis and assessment in autism*, pp. 91–110. New York: Plenum Press.

Wolfberg, P.J. (2003). *Peer play and the autism spectrum: The art of guiding children's socialization and imagination.* Shawnee Mission, KS: Autism Asperger Publishing.

MINISTRY OF EDUCATION

07-212
ISBN 978-1-4249-4957-1 (Print)
ISBN 978-1-4249-4958-8 (PDF)
ISBN 978-1-4249-4959-5 (TXT)

Printed on recycled paper